Mullahs, Guards, and *Bonyads*

An Exploration of Iranian Leadership Dynamics

David E. Thaler, Alireza Nader, Shahram Chubin,

Jerrold D. Green, Charlotte Lynch, Frederic Wehrey

Prepared for the Office of the Secretary of Defense

Approved for public release; distribution unlimited

NATIONAL DEFENSE RESEARCH INSTITUTE

The research described in this report was prepared for the Office of the Secretary of Defense (OSD). The research was conducted in the RAND National Defense Research Institute, a federally funded research and development center sponsored by the OSD, the Joint Staff, the Unified Combatant Commands, the Department of the Navy, the Marine Corps, the defense agencies, and the defense Intelligence Community under Contract W74V8H-06-C-0002.

Library of Congress Cataloging-in-Publication Data is available for this publication.

ISBN 978-0-8330-4773-1

Published 2010 by the RAND Corporation
1776 Main Street, P.O. Box 2138, Santa Monica, CA 90407-2138
1200 South Hayes Street, Arlington, VA 22202-5050
4570 Fifth Avenue, Suite 600, Pittsburgh, PA 15213-2665
RAND URL: http://www.rand.org/
To order RAND documents or to obtain additional information, contact
Distribution Services: Telephone: (310) 451-7002;
Fax: (310) 451-6915; Email: order@rand.org

Preface

The Islamic Republic of Iran poses serious challenges to U.S. interests in the Middle East, and its nuclear program continues to worry, and bring condemnation and sanction from, the international community. Yet the U.S. ability to "read" the regime in Tehran and formulate appropriate policies has been handicapped by the lack of access to Iran experienced by U.S. diplomats and other citizens and by what many observers lament as the opacity of Iranian decisionmaking processes. The objective of this book is to offer a framework to help U.S. policymakers and analysts better understand existing and evolving leadership dynamics driving Iranian decisionmaking. The research herein provides not only a basic primer on the structure, institutions, and personalities of the government and other influential power centers but also a better understanding of Iranian elite behavior as a driver of Iranian policy formulation and execution. The book pays special attention to emerging fissures within the regime, competing centers of power, and the primacy of informal networks—a particularly important yet not well understood hallmark of the Iranian system.

While our aim is to expand analysts' understanding of Iran so as to help them interpret the machinations of the country's elites, we have a profound appreciation of the complexity and historical impenetrability of Iran's political system. The motivations and behavior of the Iranian political elite have been the subject of numerous books and articles over the past several decades. One of the attributes of Iranian elite dynamics is the fact that the rules of the game are constantly in flux and are nowhere codified. Although participants certainly know the rules, for outside observers to understand them is naturally difficult. We therefore admit our ability to paint no more than a partial picture of the Iranian system. We do, however, hope to add substance, interpretation, and nuance to Western understanding of policymaking in the Islamic Republic of Iran. Our overall goal is to provide insight into the character of the Iranian "system," not to detail the pieces and interrelationships themselves.

The bulk of the research for this book was completed before the momentous Iranian presidential election of June 12, 2009, and its aftermath. The election appears to have heralded a sea change in Iranian leadership dynamics that will play out over months and years. At the time of writing in summer 2009, it is too early to determine the full ramifications of street protests challenging the election results and the government crackdown. Nevertheless, Iran's political system appears to be in a state of flux. Previously a somewhat consensus-driven system with the Supreme Leader acting as an "arbiter" above the factional fray, Iran appears to be moving toward a more authoritarian system in which Ayatollah Ali Khamenei and a small inner circle composed of close advisors and senior Revolutionary Guards members make key decisions. Where possible, we attempt to add postelection context to our analysis. However, a full understanding of the extent and nature of change in the system will be left to future research.

This research was sponsored by the Department of Defense and conducted within the Intelligence Policy Center of the RAND National Defense Research Institute, a federally funded research and development center sponsored by the Office of the Secretary of Defense, the Joint Staff, the Unified Combatant Commands, the Department of the Navy, the Marine Corps, the defense agencies, and the defense Intelligence Community. For more information on RAND's Intelligence Policy Center, contact the Director, John Parachini. He can be reached by email at John_Parachini@rand.org; by phone at 703-413-1100, extension 5579; or by mail at the RAND Corporation, 1200 South Hayes Street, Arlington, Virginia 22202-5050. More information about RAND is available at www.rand.org.

Contents

Figures

Summary

The Islamic Republic of Iran is now perceived by many as a rising power in the Middle East and a long-term challenge to U.S. regional interests. The fall of Iran's archenemy, Saddam Hussein, has enabled it to expand its influence in Iraq and beyond. Its nuclear program continues relatively unabated, with the Islamic Republic defying international condemnation and sanction to pursue an ostensibly civilian nuclear program—a program that could, technically, provide Tehran with a "breakout" capacity for nuclear arms, if it is not already a cover for a dedicated military effort. President Mahmoud Ahmadinejad has fueled the fire through his inflammatory rhetoric about the United States, its allies in the Persian Gulf region, and Israel and through his systematic denial of the Holocaust. And the presidential election in June 2009—after which the government's quick declaration of a landslide Ahmadinejad victory was challenged as fraudulent by reformist candidate Mir Hossein Mousavi and a wide array of opposition groups endured a government crackdown—presents yet another cause for U.S. and Western concern.

Yet the U.S. ability to gauge the extent and totality of the challenges posed by Iran is handicapped by the lack of official relations between the two states since 1980. Moreover, observers of the Iranian regime, both within Iran and abroad, often lament the opacity of Iranian decisionmaking processes, which presents serious impediments not only to those observers trying to understand the Iranian system and the policies it produces but even to average Iranians themselves. U.S. policymakers need both a more complete picture of the driving characteristics of the Iranian regime than they currently have and a framework to appropriately interpret Tehran's words and actions and formulate effective policies for securing U.S. interests vis-à-vis the Islamic Republic.

The objective of this book is to offer a framework to help U.S. policymakers and analysts better understand existing and evolving leadership dynamics driving Iranian decisionmaking. The research herein provides not only a basic primer on the structure, institutions, and personalities of the Iranian government and other influential power centers but also a better understanding of the strategic culture underlying Iranian policy formulation and execution. Our overall goal is to provide insight into the character of the Iranian system, not to detail the pieces and interrelationships themselves.

Iranian Strategic Culture: Views of Itself and the World

The elite of the Islamic Republic of Iran perceive Iran as the natural, indispensable, and leading power of the Middle East, even of the Muslim world. Iran's perception of its own unique centrality is informed by a strong sense of Iranian identity and by its awareness of its role as one of the region's historical powers. Iran's sense of pride and importance is influenced by feelings of victimization, insecurity, and inferiority arising from historical exploitation by outside powers. The Iranian view of the United States as the successor to British imperial rule was shaped by the 1953 Anglo-American coup that ousted Prime Minister Mohammad Mossadegh and returned Mohammad Reza Shah Pahlavi to power. This perception is still an important factor in shaping and driving Iran's strategic culture and worldview. The Islamic Republic now views the United States as its main adversary and as a threat to the regime's survival.

Iran's perception of itself is shaped by a long history of victory and defeat; it sees itself as a once-great power humbled and humiliated by the West, particularly the United States. The Islamic Revolution enhanced Iran's sense of exceptionalism and created a potent mixture of religious ideology and deep-seated nationalism. The Islamic Republic today has the ability to act beyond the confines of the revolution as a nation pursuing nonideological state interests, but its viewpoints and behavior continue to be shaped by the country's tortured history and identity as a revisionist and revolutionary state.

Key Observations on How the Iranian Political System Works

The Iranian system is one in which the informal trumps the formal, power and influence derive as much (if not more) from personality as from position, and domestic factional dynamics drive policy debates and policymaking. The system is much more than just the institutions authorized in the country's constitution. A peculiarly Iranian style of checks and balances—one that is undergoing change in the aftermath of the 2009 election—ensures that no one faction becomes so dominant as to challenge the Supreme Leader, Khamenei. There are purposeful bifurcations between the elected and the unelected and between the formal and the informal. The Supreme Leader traditionally has stood as a powerful arbiter over competing power centers, ensuring his stature by demonstrating his apparent aloofness from the fray yet entering that fray when required. However, Khamenei's decisive declaration of support for Ahmadinejad after the 2009 election has irreparably harmed Khamenei's position as an arbiter and may have significantly decreased his credibility among Iran's diverse power centers.

The System: Personalities, Informal Networks, Institutions

The system is a composite of key personalities, their informal networks and relationships with other individuals and power centers, and the institutions with which these personalities are associated. A number of key individuals (including, first and foremost, Khamenei) have dominated the political elite in Iran, largely since the 1979 revolution and certainly since the death of the father of the revolution, Ayatollah Ruhollah Khomeini, a decade later. These personalities draw on multiple networks of various commonalities—interleaved family, experiential, clerical, political, financial, and other relationships and interests—that serve as levers of patronage, mobilization, and dissent.

Lastly, individuals use their positions in institutions to acquire financial wealth and to become sources of patronage, thereby empowering their own families, allies, and networks. The more powerful, influential, and well-connected the individual or individuals leading an institution are, the greater the weight that institution gains in policymaking and implementation within Iran. In sum, it is the *combination* of key personalities, networks based on a number of commonalities, and institutions—not any one of these elements alone—that defines the political system of the Islamic Republic.

The Supreme Leader Retains the Most Power, but He Is Not Omnipotent

Khamenei is the most powerful and influential individual in Iran. His power derives from a number of sources, including his own broad networks of representatives, appointees, and confidantes; his role as commander in chief; and his very position as Supreme Leader. But, lacking Khomeini's iconic status and charisma, Khamenei must balance a multitude of competing interests to ensure that no single faction or group becomes so dominant that it threatens his power and prerogatives. This means operating in what is a relatively dysfunctional political system that tends toward stasis and where the absence of forward movement and innovation in the system is normal. "Balance" among interest groups is the guarantor of the Supreme Leader's indispensability. However, recently, he acts less like an even-handed arbiter and more like a participant in the rivalries among individuals, groups, and factions. He shows a preference for ideological and social conservatives, considering them authentic revolutionaries and his natural allies. He welcomes "resistance" against the United States and the West as long as the risks of confrontation are contained.

Factional Competition Drives Political Discourse and Policymaking

The Supreme Leader encourages factional rivalry as long as it does not threaten the system. The factions in turn operate within the limits needed to preserve the Islamic regime, but survival of the regime is the point at which the so-called consensus ends. Factional maneuvering is a key manifestation of the competition for power and influence, and foreign- and domestic-policy issues are used as tools and are extensions of this competition.

Factions use foreign policy to promote their domestic agendas. For example, Mohammad Khatami and the reformists pursued normalization and a "dialogue of civilizations" to open Iranian society, and Ahmadinejad and his factional allies have pursued confrontation as an excuse to restrict it. Factional differences over foreign and domestic policies are, at their core, an ongoing battle between fundamentally different views of what Iran should become. This battle engenders a debate about the essence of the state and the legitimacy and staying power of the Islamic Revolution. Contention between the two visions—one emphasizing the Islamic *Revolution* and a model of resistance and self-sufficiency, the other emphasizing the Islamic *Republic* and a model of normalcy and independent development—will endure for years to come. At the time of writing in summer 2009, the revolutionary mind-set appeared to be ascendant.

Iran's Domestic Power Politics Are Highly Dynamic and Periodic

In each of the three decades since the revolution, a different power center has been more influential than others. During the Khomeini era and the Iran-Iraq War, the clerics appeared to enjoy a period of primacy. The 1990s were the era of economic dominance of the *bonyads* (parastatal foundations), with the clerics continuing to wield considerable political influence. The Islamic Revolutionary Guard Corps (IRGC) appears to have dominated during the first decade of the millennium, using Iran's increased emphasis on security issues as a political and economic lever. A new generation of lay leaders with an IRGC pedigree—Ahmadinejad, Ali Larijani, Mohammad Baqer Qalibaf, and others—has arisen to pose a challenge to clerics and to the "old guard." In the 1980s and 1990s, the most-valuable connections were ties with the clerics, but now they are ties with the Revolutionary Guards. The IRGC and the Basij increasingly insert themselves into politics and business. However, as with any power center in Iran, the IRGC is not monolithic. Senior commanders appointed by the Supreme Leader may be revolutionary "fire-breathers," but others among the rank-and-file (including those who fought in the Iran-Iraq War) may be more representative of the larger society of Iran, with many of the latter espousing a more pragmatic view of the world.

Emerging Trends to Watch in Iran

Our research identified three trends that appear to be emerging as key determinants of the future direction of the Islamic Republic of Iran.

The Revolutionary Guards: Will They Rise or Fall?

As the third decade of the Islamic Revolution comes to a close, the future role of the IRGC arises as a key question. The Guards appear to have played a major role in ensuring an Ahmadinejad victory in the June 2009 presidential election. The IRGC is a major domestic political, economic, and security power center, and active members and alumni pervade the government and other sectors of society. A spectrum of mind-sets has emerged within the IRGC vis-à-vis the environment in which the organization operates. One view is more security-conscious, with holders of this mind-set seeing the existence of a geostrategic battle between Iran and the United States for power and influence in the region and wanting to pursue confrontation to secure the "rights" of Iran and the survival of the Islamic Revolution. Others in the IRGC are more profit-oriented and are focused on securing lucrative business ventures. Although they agree that Iran is engaged in a strategic competition with the United States, they believe that the rivalry between the two countries can be eased in the name of a more positive commercial environment.

What future might evolve from this situation? If the Guards continue to gain political power, they could begin to see themselves as kingmakers and demand more from the Supreme Leader and the clerics. Or, the IRGC may—especially if it is at the apex of its domestic influence when Khamenei dies—make a bid for power in the next several years, possibly even challenging the Assembly of Experts in selecting the next Supreme Leader. This second scenario could be quite worrisome if the Islamic Republic were to attain the capacity to build and deploy nuclear weapons. Alternatively, an increase in the IRGC's focus on economic power could lead it to become an institution that is profit driven, bureaucratic, less flexible, and more risk averse. A focus on business and profits could cause the IRGC to see greater utility in regional stability and reduced tensions with the United States and the West.

The Old Guard: Vulnerable to Challenge?

A second trend to watch over the next few years is the evolution of the relationship between the older generation, which overthrew the Shah and brought Khomeini to power, and a younger cohort of lay leaders (with some clerical allies) who were shaped primarily by the early years of the Islamic Republic and are less beholden to the older establishment. The leaders of the older generation are entrenched politically and financially and do not retire voluntarily from politics. Yet, as gatekeepers, they have been instrumental in admitting the younger generation into the governing elite. The new generation of "revolutionary" leaders is seeking to carve out independent centers of power and influence, sometimes in ways that may challenge the positions and power of their elders. Ahmadinejad's populist outreach to the rural and urban underclasses and his public accusations against "economic mafias" can be partially understood in this context. At some point in the future, the older generation will pass naturally from the scene. The question is whether its members will be forced out before that time and, if so, what this might mean for the Iranian system. Clearly, the Islamic Republic's traditional elites have survived past internal challenges by remaining unified when under threat and by adapting to or co-opting countervailing political and social trends.

The Next Supreme Leader: Who or What Will Succeed Khamenei?

By 2009, Khamenei will have held the position of Supreme Leader for two-thirds of the Islamic Republic's existence. He will have guided Iran through periods of tension and momentous change in its neighborhood and through international condemnation and isolation over its nuclear program. But he turned 70 years old in 2009, and rumors about his deteriorating health have recently surfaced. The nature of the succession when he passes from the scene will be difficult to predict. Will the transition be smooth, or will it be marked by conflict that destabilizes the system? What kind of successor will be selected, and how might the office of Supreme Leader evolve?

The next Supreme Leader will be a primary determinant of how the other two trends evolve. The scope of his power and the level of his influence within the system will be critical factors in determining Iran's future direction, particularly with regard to relations with the United States and with other states in the region. A relatively strong leader may continue the status quo or steer the country toward gradual change (for ill or good, depending on one's perspective), whereas a weak leader could be exploited or dominated by other power centers, such as the IRGC. In the latter case, the very nature of the Islamic Republic could change drastically and in potentially destabilizing ways. In our view, therefore, the internal discussions and activities surrounding the succession of the Supreme Leader constitute the most important development for U.S. and Western policymakers and analysts to watch as a harbinger of the future direction of the Islamic Republic.

Selected Thoughts for U.S. Policymakers

The United States and its presence in the Middle East are a key focus of Iranian decisionmakers. The Iranian elite keenly observes U.S. official statements and other signals toward Iran. The elite's interpretation of these signals shapes Iran's foreign, and at times domestic, policies. In fact, Washington's responses to statements or posturing from Tehran can enhance the importance of an issue in internal Iranian debates beyond its inherent relevance. It is therefore incumbent on U.S. policymakers to couch their communications with and about Iran in ways that are nuanced and that consider how such statements might be perceived in Tehran (and by whom). The United States is at a distinct disadvantage because its diplomats and citizens lack broad access to the Islamic Republic and, thus, to intimate knowledge of its inner workings.

If Iranian relations with the United States and the international community become more normalized in the future, U.S. policymakers must take as an article of faith that dealing with Iran does not necessarily mean dealing with a unitary actor. Normal relations with the United States would be a radical departure for Iran's elites, and they would need to recognize and accept these relations as necessary both for Iran (and for preservation of the Islamic Revolution) *and* their own power and influence (and that of the patronage networks upon which they rely). Factional politics make openings for dialogue and a stable U.S.-Iranian relationship difficult, as do Iran's competing government structures and power centers. Increased engagement with the United States and the West would have domestic consequences for Iran and create winners and losers, and the latter would not necessarily acquiesce willingly, even if the Supreme Leader fully supported such engagement. One key for the United States is to enter dialogue with Iran armed with a nuanced view of the complex system of government and politics that the Iranian interlocutors across the negotiating table represent.

Acknowledgments

The authors wish to thank a number of people for their support of the research that informed this book. First, many thanks go to Erik Olson for his guidance and insights as the sponsor of the project. The authors also wish to thank John Parachini and Kathi Webb, Director and Associate Director, respectively, of the RAND Intelligence Policy Center, for their encouragement and patient oversight of the study.

The authors also would like to express great appreciation for the time and insights of a number of top Iran scholars in the United States and elsewhere. These contributions were extremely valuable, and without them, the research that led to this book would not have been possible. The authors engaged these scholars in very-fruitful discussions about informal networks in Iran in an effort to gain greater understanding of the Iranian system. Many of these scholars preferred to remain anonymous because of the sensitive nature of their activities.

The authors offer profound gratitude to John Limbert, Professor of International Affairs, United States Naval Academy, and Daniel Byman, Director of the Security Studies Program and the Center for Peace and Security Studies, Georgetown University, for their thoughtful formal reviews of an earlier manuscript. Their comments greatly enhanced the substance of the book. Also, the authors thank Karim Sadjadpour, Associate, Carnegie Endowment for International Peace, for his insights on some of the concepts included in the analysis.

Finally, the authors would like to thank RAND colleagues Lydia Hansell and Francisco Walter for their help with citations and manuscript preparation, Gail Kouril and Ahmad Rahmani for tracking down numerous Iranian media references, and Erin-Elizabeth Johnson for her thorough edit of the document.

Of course, the content of this book is solely the responsibility of the authors.

Abbreviations

AoE	Assembly of Experts
EC	Expediency Council
EU	European Union
EU3	Great Britain, France, and Germany
GCC	Gulf Cooperation Council
IAEA	International Atomic Energy Agency
IRGC	Islamic Revolutionary Guard Corps
LEF	Law Enforcement Forces
MOIS	Ministry of Intelligence and Security
NIE	National Intelligence Estimate
SCFR	Strategic Council for Foreign Relations
SNSC	Supreme National Security Council
UAE	United Arab Emirates
UFC	uranium-conversion facility
UN	United Nations

CHAPTER ONE

Introduction: Leadership Dynamics in the Islamic Republic of Iran

Since the election of Mahmoud Ahmadinejad as president of the Islamic Republic of Iran in 2005, Iran's regional ambitions and its confrontation with the international community over its nuclear program have made it one of the most pressing foreign-policy issues for the United States. The Islamic Republic is widely assumed to be pursuing a nuclear-weapon capability, and its influence in the Persian Gulf region, Iraq, Lebanon, and elsewhere appears to be on the rise. Iran poses a significant challenge to U.S. interests and to those of U.S. allies in the region. After reviewing a range of global threats, the 2006 *National Security Strategy of the United States of America* warns, "We may face no greater challenge from a single country than from Iran."[1] More recently, President Barack Obama stated that Iran's "actions over many years now . . . create the possibility of destabilizing the region and are not only contrary to our interests, but I think are contrary to the interests of international peace."[2] Over time, much of the international community has come to accept the U.S. view of the Islamic Republic as a danger to peace and stability. The 2009 presidential-election dispute and the resulting crackdowns on the largely peaceful protests have added to these concerns.

---

[1] The White House, *The National Security Strategy of the United States of America*, Washington, D.C., March 2006, p. 1.

[2] Barack Obama, "Press Conference by the President," Washington, D.C., February 9, 2009.

Yet the U.S. ability to gauge the extent and totality of the challenges posed by Iran has been handicapped by the lack of official relations between the two states since the Islamic Revolution of 1979. Nearly 30 years of U.S.-Iranian estrangement and the absence of a U.S. diplomatic presence in Tehran have severely limited Washington's access to Iranian political elites. Few if any members of today's U.S. policymaking community have visited Iran since 1979, leading to a superficial understanding of the country, its politics, and its society.[3] Moreover, and perhaps more importantly, observers of the Iranian regime often lament the opacity of Iranian decisionmaking processes, which presents serious impediments not only to those outside observers trying to understand the Iranian system and the policies it produces but even to average Iranians themselves. If they are to pursue U.S. interests vis-à-vis Iran to the fullest extent, U.S. policymakers and analysts require a more comprehensive picture of the key characteristics of Iranian decisionmaking than they currently have.

The objective of this book is to offer a framework to help U.S. policymakers and analysts better understand existing and evolving leadership dynamics driving Iranian decisionmaking, appropriately interpret Tehran's words and actions, and formulate effective policies for securing U.S. interests vis-à-vis the Islamic Republic. The research described herein provides not only a basic primer on the structure, institutions, and personalities of the Iranian government and other influential power centers but also a better understanding of factors that drive Iranian policy formulation and execution. This book pays special attention to emerging fissures within the regime, competing centers of power, and the primacy of informal networks—a particularly important yet not well understood hallmark of the Iranian system. As we shall see, the informal trumps the formal in Iran as a means of gaining influence and making policy.

---

[3]   One reviewer noted that in addition to the lack of U.S. presence in Iran, U.S. government and academic programs for studying the politics and language of Iran are weak. On the other hand, there is a large Iranian diaspora, some of whose members live in the United States, which offers significant knowledge and experience.

After briefly discussing our research methodology in the remainder of this chapter, we provide in Chapter Two an assessment of the strategic culture that drives the perceptions and outlook of the Islamic Republic's leadership cadres. This culture derives from the nation's experiences (both recent and more remote), its Shi'a Islamic and Persian-dominated character, and its political status and geographical position in the region. In Chapter Three, we review the formal structures of the Islamic Republic as described in its constitution and examine how the responsibilities and authorities of these structures overlap and have evolved over time. The formal institutions serve as a playing field for cooperation and competition among various personalities and their formal and informal networks, a topic we explore in detail in Chapter Four. Informal networks are based on common experiences, outlooks, and other interests, and competition among them appears be a key driver of elite behavior in the Islamic Republic. In Chapter Five, we describe the impact of factional competition on the evolution of two of Iran's core foreign policies: (1) its policies toward its Middle Eastern neighbors and (2) its interaction with the international community regarding its nuclear program. We also indicate how the Iranian economy has become a key battleground for factional rivalry. Finally, Chapter Six suggests a lens through which U.S. decisionmakers and analysts can interpret Iranian political discourse and provides a summary of key trends.

In our research for this book, we sought to utilize unique and unusual sources that could provide insights well beyond what can be found in the Western press and in journals and other popular sources of information. We relied on input from non–RAND Corporation consultants who are among the top Iran experts inside and outside the United States and who have frequent access to key individuals and communities at diverse societal and political levels in Iran. Many such consultants have a native-level Persian-language capability. We based our discussions with these scholars on a series of questions designed to elicit insight into the crucial and often subtle informal interactions that drive elite behavior in the Islamic Republic. Generally, we asked our interlocutors to identify Iran's main informal groupings and key individuals; address how these people and groups mobilize other members to gain consensus, promote loyalty, express dissent, or obstruct other groups or policies; describe how these people and groups interact with other groups and individuals; assess how much influence the groups have; and characterize the overall paradigm under which the Iranian system works. As we held these discussions, we identified and developed common themes, reviewing them with the scholars to ensure their relevance.

Using our own Persian-language skills, we analyzed Iranian media, the statements of key leaders, Persian-language journals published by Iranian think tanks, and Persian-language policy journals. We also relied on consultations with U.S. government analysts and on previous RAND work on various aspects of Iran's security policy.[4]

---

[4]   Daniel Byman, Shahram Chubin, Anoushiravan Ehteshami, and Jerrold D. Green, *Iran's Security Policy in the Post-Revolutionary Era*, Santa Monica, Calif.: RAND Corporation, MR-1320-OSD, 2001; Frederic Wehrey, David E. Thaler, Nora Bensahel, Kim Cragin, Jerrold D. Green, Dalia Dassa Kaye, Nadia Oweidat, and Jennifer Li, *Dangerous But Not Omnipotent: Exploring the Reach and Limitations of Iranian Power in the Middle East*, Santa Monica, Calif.: RAND Corporation, MG-781-AF, 2009; Frederic Wehrey, Jerrold D. Green, Brian Nichiporuk, Alireza Nader, Lydia Hansell, Rasool Nafisi, and S. R. Bohandy, *The Rise of the Pasdaran: Assessing the Domestic Roles of the Islamic Revolutionary Guards Corps*, Santa Monica, Calif.: RAND Corporation, MG-821-OSD, 2009; Jerrold D. Green, Frederic Wehrey, and Charles Wolf, Jr., *Understanding Iran*, Santa Monica, Calif.: RAND Corporation, MG-771-SRF, 2009; Keith Crane, Rollie Lal, and Jeffrey Martini, *Iran's Political, Demographic, and Economic Vulnerabilities*, Santa Monica, Calif.: RAND Corporation, MG-693-AF, 2008.

CHAPTER TWO

Assertiveness and Caution in Iranian Strategic Culture

The elites of the Islamic Republic perceive Iran to be the natural, indispensable, and leading power of the Middle East, or even the Muslim world. Iran's perception of its own unique centrality is informed by a strong sense of Iranian identity and awareness of the country's role as one of the region's historical powers. From the time of the first Persian Empire (550–330 BC) to the present era, Iran has played a vital role in shaping the Middle East, but it has also been shaped by outside forces. Although Iran ceased to be a great power in the 18th century, its current size, population, strategic location, energy reserves, and perception of its central role in global politics propel it to claim the vital role it once played.

Feelings of victimization, insecurity, and inferiority have helped form Iran's sense of pride and importance. Initially a nation of conquerors, Iran was, over time, repeatedly invaded, conquered, and humbled by other powers, including the Greeks, the Arabs, the Mongols, and the Turks. Its perennial sense of victimization is most recently associated with the British and Russian domination of Iran from the 19th to the mid-20th centuries and with the perceived domination of Iran by the United States after the Second World War. The Iranian view of the United States as the successor to British imperial rule was shaped by the 1953 Anglo-American coup that ousted Prime Minister Mohammad Mossadegh and returned Mohammad Reza Shah Pahlavi to power. This perception is still an important factor in the minds of those who shape and drive Iranians' strategic culture and worldviews.

In this chapter, we discuss Iran's historic sense of grandeur, victimization, and domination by foreign powers, including the United States. In addition, we examine the effects of the Islamic Revolution on Iran's strategic culture, from its attempts to export the revolution to its pragmatic dealing with neighbors and outside powers. Iran's strategic culture, however, is not static: It is in a constant state of flux and evolution. Competing trends and ideas in Iran's strategic culture have facilitated political factionalism and hindered development of a coherent and consistent foreign policy.

Iran: The Conquering and Conquered Nation

Iranians view their history with immense pride—tinged with bitterness—and consider their country to be one of the world's great civilizations. The Achaemanid dynasty, which established Iran as an independent nation and ruled an empire stretching from Egypt to India, is usually cited as the herald of Iran's golden age. After its conquest by Alexander the Great, Iran became a great power again under the Iranian-dominated Parthian (247 BC–224 AD[1]) and Sassanid (224–651) dynasties. The Arab armies, having defeated the Sassanids in 651, established Islam as Iran's new religion.

The Islamic Republic's founders and stewards have a positive view of the Arab conquest. In their opinion, the arrival of Islam rescued pagan Iran from the age of ignorance; hence, Islam, rather than the bygone Persian empires, serves as the anchor of Iran's national self-image.[2] However, many more-secular and more-nationalist Iranians who are wary of the Islamic Republic view the Arab conquest of Iran as a time of humiliation and subjugation.[3] They believe that the Arab armies destroyed the thriving pre-Islamic Zoroastrian civilization that

---

[1]   Unless otherwise noted, subsequent dates are AD.

[2]   Hooshang Amirahmadi, "From Political Islam to National Secularism," Abadan Publishing Co., January 11, 2006.

[3]   Fred Halliday, "Arabs and Persians Beyond the Geopolitics of the Gulf," *Cahiers d'Études sur la Méditerranée Orientale et le Mond Turco-Iranien*, March 4, 2005.

had defined Iran and much of the Middle East for hundreds of years. Although Iran experienced renewed periods of national greatness and regional power after the Arab conquest, especially under the Safavids (1502–1736) and, some might argue, under the Pahlavi dynasty (1925–1979), it never regained the unquestioned status of a regional superpower that it had enjoyed before the Arab conquest.

The Safavid dynasty established Shi'ism as the dominant Islamic sect in Iran and created the greatest Iranian empire that had existed since the Arab conquest. The Safavids rivaled the Ottoman Empire in regional influence and managed to extend Iranian rule over much of Iraq, Afghanistan, and the Caucasus.[4] The succeeding Qajar dynasty (1795–1925) oversaw Iran's gradual decline and dominance by Western powers.

Under the Qajars, Iran became entangled in the tug of war between the expanding British and Russian empires. Russian forays into the Caucasus and Central Asia, which had been a traditional sphere of Iranian influence, led to the Russo-Persian War of 1804–1813.[5] Iran was soundly defeated and forced to cede Georgia and much of the Caucasus to Russian rule in the Treaty of Gulistan (1813).[6] Weakened by this defeat, Iran soon fell prey to Great Britain's imperial ambitions. Iran's attempt to reclaim the Afghan city of Herat led both to its defeat in the Anglo-Persian War (1856–1857)[7] and its loss of influence in Afghanistan and the surrounding region. The Reuters Concession of 1872, which granted the British virtual control over Iran's national resources in return for payments to the Shah's government,[8] and the Anglo-Persian agreement of 1919,[9] which authorized British control

---

[4] Halliday, 2005.

[5] Encyclopædia Britannica Online, "Treaty of Golestān," *Encyclopædia Britannica*, no date available.

[6] Encyclopædia Britannica Online, no date available.

[7] John Carl Nelson, *The Siege of Herat 1837–1838*, thesis, St. Cloud, Minn.: St. Cloud State University, 1976.

[8] Nikki Eddie, *Modern Iran: Roots and Results of a Revolution*, New Haven, Conn.: Yale University Press, 2006, p. 72.

[9] A. R. Begli Beigie, "Repeating Mistakes: Britain, Iran & the 1919 Treaty," *The Iranian*, March 27, 2001.

over Iranian oil, became enduring symbols of Iran's subservience to Western powers. The roles of Great Britain and Russia in suppressing Iran's democratic Constitutional Revolution of 1905—support that worked in the Shah's favor—were also a reminder that Iran's people had little say in their own destiny.[10]

Iranian resentment of what it considers to be a history of Western domination and imperialism can be traced to this era of quasicolonial domination. The "dismemberment" of Iran's territory and Iran's loss of regional power wounded the Iranian national psyche for years to come. More importantly, the Qajar shahs were viewed as the instruments of foreign powers and perceived as willing to compromise Iran's sovereignty for personal gain.

The Pahlavi monarchs did not fare much better. Although some Iranians saw Reza Shah Pahlavi as a true nationalist and a great modernizer, others, including much of the clergy, viewed him as an instrument of Western culture and virulently opposed his efforts to "de-Islamicize" Iran by banning the *hejab*, the modest dress worn by religious Muslim women.[11] Due to his support for Nazi Germany during the Second World War, Reza Shah Pahlavi was deposed by invading British and Soviet forces in 1941 and replaced by his son, Mohammad Reza Shah Pahlavi.[12]

Mohammad Reza fled Iran after the democratically elected government of Mossadegh challenged him, but he was restored to power by a 1953 coup organized by the United States and Great Britain. Much like the Qajar shahs, Mohammad Reza was viewed as a proxy serving British and, later, U.S. interests. As was the case with his father's initiatives, the efforts of Mohammad Reza (hereafter referred to as the Shah) to modernize Iran were viewed by large segments of the population, particularly the clergy, as an attempt to impose Western culture on Islamic Iran. More importantly, many Iranians viewed the Shah

---

[10] Younes Parsa Benab, "The Origin and Development of Imperialist Contention in Iran; 1884–1921," Iran Chamber Society, June 11, 2008.

[11] Shahrough Akhavi, *Religion and Politics in Contemporary Iran: Clergy-State Relations in the Pahlavi Period*, Albany, N.Y.: State University of New York Press, 1980.

[12] Iran Chamber Society, "Reza Shah Pahlavi," Web page, undated.

as serving U.S. regional interests rather than Iran's national interests. Dubbed by some as the "guardian" of the Persian Gulf, the Shah was considered a key pillar of the U.S.-supported security regime in the Persian Gulf and the Middle East. Although the Shah considered himself and Iran to be indispensable to regional security, many Iranians viewed him as being unable to make strategic decisions without U.S. approval. In addition, many Iranians resented the United States for buttressing what they considered to be the Shah's undemocratic and repressive regime.

National pride, a sense of victimization, and fears of foreign domination continue to dominate Iran's strategic culture and behavior. Significant segments of the Iranian population continue to believe that Iran's natural place as a regional power is jeopardized by U.S. and, perhaps, even British interests and actions. Iran's ruling elite not only appears to share this belief but consistently takes advantage of it to justify assertive domestic and foreign policies.

Nationalism as a Tool of Policy

The Islamic Republic views the United States as its main existential threat. The 1979 takeover of the U.S. embassy in Tehran was in part motivated by fears that Washington would bring the Shah back to power. Many Iranians believe that Washington authorized Saddam Hussein's invasion of Iran in 1980 as retribution for the overthrow of the Shah. Suspicion of the United States among the Islamic Republic's elite persists to this day. The U.S. invasions of Afghanistan (2001) and Iraq (2003) aggravated the regime's fears of U.S. domination, especially because those countries could be used to initiate regime change in Iran. Tehran at first reacted cautiously to the U.S. invasion of Afghanistan, but it later played an active and at times helpful role in establishing the post-Taliban government of Hamid Karzai.[13] However, U.S. rhetoric toward Iran and the invasion of Iraq in 2003 greatly increased Tehran's suspicion of Washington's intentions, and the George W. Bush administration's Greater Middle East agenda was seen as a plot to bring the

---

[13] "Iran Welcomes Bonn Agreement on Afghanistan Despite Its 'Weak Points,'" Islamic Republic News Agency, December 7, 2001. See also James Dobbins, "Negotiating with Iran," in Green, Wehrey, and Wolf, 2009, pp. 66–70.

Middle East, including Iran, under U.S. domination. Many within the elite viewed Iran's inclusion in the so-called axis of evil as an indication of hostile U.S. intentions, including the invasion of Iran and the overthrow of the Islamic Republic.

Iran's government began to view an invasion as increasingly unlikely the more it perceived U.S. forces as becoming bogged down in what it considered to be the "quagmire" of Iraq and Afghanistan. At the same time, Iranian officials promoted the belief that the United States was intent on regime change through a secretly organized velvet revolution of the kind that had overthrown the ruling regimes in Serbia, Ukraine, and Georgia.[14] Furthermore, these officials depicted the George W. Bush administration's establishment of an Iran democracy fund as an effort to organize a soft coup in Iran, much like the coup that had taken place in 1953.[15]

It is not clear how much of the Iranian population believed the government's rhetoric regarding the velvet revolution; nevertheless, the rhetoric provided the Ahmadinejad administration with the justification to further suppress internal dissent and pursue enforcement of morality laws. Fears of a velvet revolution were also used as a pretext in the arrest and imprisonment of five Iranian-Americans visiting Iran for various reasons, the most prominent of whom was Haleh Esfandiari of the Woodrow Wilson International Center.[16] In addition, Iran's minister of intelligence, Gholam-Hussein Mohseni-Ejei, warned Iranian academics to avoid U.S.-sponsored educational seminars and conferences, which he claimed were designed to train them as "spies."[17] These events led some prominent Iranian democracy activists to openly renounce U.S. democracy funding for Iran.[18]

---

[14] Jesse Nunes, "Iran Detains Two on Accusations of Plotting Velvet Revolution," *Christian Science Monitor*, May 23, 2007.

[15] Negar Azimi, "Hard Realities of Soft Power," *Iran Emrooz* (Tehran), June 24, 2007.

[16] Nunes, 2007.

[17] "Iranian Intelligence Ministry Closely Monitoring Foreigners' Subversive Activities: Minister," Mehr News Agency, July 3, 2007.

[18] Golnaz Esfandiari, "Iran: Political Activists to Steer Clear of Possible U.S. Funding," Radio Free Europe/Radio Liberty, April 4, 2008.

The Iranian government also accused the United States and Great Britain of plotting to "dismember" Iran by aiding ethnic insurgent and separatist groups, such as the Baluchis in the southeast, the Arabs in the southwest, and the Kurds in the northwest. According to Iran's former national security advisor, Ali Larijani, "the United States has become so weak that it is trying to strengthen groups like Pejak and others to carry out actions like blowing up oil pipelines in Iran."[19] Whether true or false, such accusations may resonate among Iranians inured to a culture of foreign oppression and domination. The British were previously known for using Iranian tribes and ethnic groups, including the Baluchis, to weaken Iran's central government and authority. In the minds of the Iranian leadership, why would Great Britain's imperial successor, the United States, act otherwise?

The Obama administration's offer to engage in constructive dialogue with the Islamic Republic without preconditions has appeared to alter the dynamic within the regime. Obama's messages to the regime and the Iranian people, and the change in U.S. policy that such messages represented, were front and center in the campaigns and debates leading up to Iran's June 2009 presidential election. The new U.S. policy will limit the ability of the Iranian government both to portray the United States as a bogeyman bent on destabilizing the regime and to garner popular support through such rhetoric.

Iran's leaders, though not proponents of Iranian nationalism per se, have used the population's sense of patriotism and suspicion to gain greater support for their policies in the Middle East.[20] Iranian sensitivities regarding national sovereignty are apparent in the dispute between Iran and the United Arab Emirates (UAE) over the ownership of the Tunb and Abu Musa islands in the Persian Gulf. The islands, which

---

[19] "Iran Accuses U.S. of Supporting Rebel Groups," Agence France-Presse, September 6, 2007.

[20] For example, the claim by Hoseyn Shariatmadari, editor of the prominent conservative newspaper *Kayhan* that Bahrain was a part of "Islamic" Iran may have been met with nods of approval by many Iranians who believe that Bahrain was "separated" from Iran "through an illicit conformity between the former Shah and the governments of Britain and United States" ("Iran Stakes Claim to Bahrain: Public Seeks 'Reunification . . . with Its Motherland,'" WorldTribune.com, July 13, 2007).

were occupied by the Shah after the British departed in 1971, are seen by Iran as an "inseparable" and "intrinsic part of Iranian territory," and any discussion of their return to the UAE is seen as an affront to Iranian sovereignty.[21]

Continuing efforts to rename the Persian Gulf the *Arabian Gulf* has also produced much nationalist angst in Iran. The effort has become a useful rallying cry for the government and has led to official denunciations and organized demonstrations. Following GoogleEarth's use of *Arabian Gulf* on its maps and rising tensions between Iran and the UAE regarding the disputed Tunb and Abu Musa islands, Iranian Expediency Council Chairman Ali Akbar Hashemi Rafsanjani stated that "there are valid documents about the Persian Gulf in religious and historical books, especially commentaries on the Holy Quran; therefore, no country has the right to alter the name."[22] Interestingly, Rafsanjani justified the use of the nationalist term *Persian Gulf* by citing Islamic sources, demonstrating a skillful blending of nationalist and Islamist ideology.

The nuclear issue is also couched in nationalist and religious themes. Iranian government and religious leaders have repeatedly claimed that "it is self-evident in Islam that it is prohibited to have nuclear bombs. It is eternal law, because the basic function of these weapons is to kill innocent people. This cannot be reversed."[23] By stating that nuclear weapons are forbidden, Iranian officials, including Ayatollah Ali Khamenei, can portray Washington's attempt to hinder Tehran's nuclear program as motivated by opposition to Iran's technological advancement. Khamenei's attitude is typical among the Iranian elite: It is formed not only by a nationalistic sense of foreign oppression

[21] "Iran Deplores UAE Claim on 3 Islands," *Islamic Republic News Agency*, April 17, 2008.

[22] Akbar Hashemi Rafsanjani, "'Persian Gulf' Is the Historical Name," *Tehran Times*, April 30, 2008c.

[23] Grand Ayatollah Yusef Saanei, quoted in Robert Collier, "Nuclear Weapons Unholy, Iran Says," *San Francisco Chronicle*, October 31, 2003.

but also by a revolutionary ideology that sees Iran and the world of Islam as victims of U.S. power.[24]

A New Revolutionary Paradigm

The Islamic Revolution of 1979 greatly influenced Iran's strategic culture and identity by formalizing its sense of victimization while introducing a radical Shi'a ideology of *moqavamat* [resistance] against *zolm* [injustice]. The revolution was in large part a reaction to the Shah's autocracy and perceived subservience to foreign powers, especially the United States. However, the revolution's leaders struggled not only against the Shah but also against what they saw as global injustice perpetrated by the United States. Although the revolution's distinctive religious and nationalist components were Shi'a and Iranian respectively, Iran's leaders proudly viewed their revolution as belonging to the entire world—or at a minimum, to the entire Islamic world.

Iran's revolutionary leaders have historically perceived the world of international politics as both unjust and organized to favor the interests of the great powers, notably the United States. In this view, the world order is exclusive and fails to recognize the independence of non-Western powers.[25] In his speech at the 61st annual session of the United Nations (UN) General Assembly, Ahmadinejad remarked that

> certain powers equate themselves with the international community and whose decisions are to be controlling [sic] over those of 180 others. They consider themselves the masters and rulers of the entire world while other nations should be content with only second class status [in this world order].[26]

---

[24] This attitude of victimization is similar to the argument made by many Iranian royalists that the United States and its allies brought down the Shah because they feared he was making Iran too powerful.

[25] Ali Larijani, "Speech at the 43rd Munich Conference on Security Policy," Munich Security Conference, February 11, 2007a.

[26] "Address to the UN," Islamic Republic News Agency, September 26, 2007d.

Ahmadinejad and other Iranian leaders view the United States as maintaining the global status quo, and hence it is with the United States that the Islamic Republic has been inordinately preoccupied.

The Islamic Republic's elites attribute the United States' intrinsic enmity towards Iran (of which they are convinced) to three factors: first, the Islamic character of Iran's system; second, Iran's insistence on independence (as opposed to the Shah's willingness to supinely follow orders); and, third, the energy resources in the region, which the United States seeks to control and dominate.[27] Such a view may preclude any compromise, as the problems between Iran and the United States appear to be fundamental and extensive; after all, senior figures within the Iranian government, including Khamenei, believe that the United States opposes the Islamic Republic's very existence, not to mention its national independence.[28]

Exporting the Revolution

Just as Iran's Islamist revolutionaries believed that the Shah's overthrow had rescued Iran from an unjust international system, so too did they see a requirement to free fellow Muslims from the grip of perceived reactionary forces (in particular, Arab authoritarian regimes) allied with the United States. To liberate its coreligionists and defend its own revolution from the United States, the Iranian government initially began to form and aid like-minded groups, such as Lebanese Hezbollah, in an effort to bring the Islamic Revolution to the rest of the region. Closer to home, Iranian agents were directly implicated in a 1981 coup attempt against the government of Bahrain by the Islamic

---

[27] For a typical example, see Ayatollah Ali Khamenei's address to the students at Shahid Beheshti University, May 2003, quoted in Karim Sadjadpour, *Reading Khamenei: The World View of Iran's Most Powerful Leader*, Washington, D.C.: Carnegie Endowment for International Peace, 2008, p. 14.

[28] Arguably, many of the reformists and so-called pragmatists disagree with this view of the United States. Obama's election to the presidency has raised hopes among some Iranians of a détente between the United States and the Islamic Republic. The Obama administration may be seen as a valuable interlocutor by moderate and pragmatic segments of the Iranian elite. However, conservative figures in Iran are wary of engaging the United States because such engagement could lead to stronger internal demands for political, economic, and social reforms.

Front for the Liberation of Bahrain, and they were accused of supporting Shi'a revolutionaries in Iraq and Saudi Arabia.[29]

With the exception of Hezbollah, Iran's efforts to expand its ideology and revolution beyond its borders were unsuccessful. The Iraqi Shi'as, influenced by the nonpolitical quietist trend in Shi'a Islam and by Arab nationalism, rejected the Iranian principle of *velayat-e faqih* [rule of the jurisprudent, a concept that Ayatollah Ruhollah Khomeini introduced] and even fought against Iranian forces during the Iran-Iraq War (1980–1988). In addition, the majority of Arab Shi'as in the Persian Gulf states remained loyal to their rulers. If anything, Iran's attempts to export its revolution may have weakened the Islamic Republic's ideological appeal and led to Iran's increased isolation, both regionally and globally. The Gulf Cooperation Council (GCC) was formed in 1981 in part to respond to the Iranian threat, and Hussein's Iraq received massive financial and material support from the GCC states, especially Saudi Arabia, during its long war with Iran.[30]

The Arab reaction to the revolution and Iran's isolation during the Iran-Iraq War arguably enhanced Iran's sense of exceptionalism in the region and in the international system.[31] Khomeini's interpretation of *velayat-e faqih* as the foundation of the political system has remained unique to Iran to this day. However, the Islamic Republic's foreign-policy failures during its first decade of existence also ushered in a period of pragmatism and moderation, especially after the death of Khomeini in 1989. Whereas Khomeini had favored the export of the Islamic Revolution, subsequent Iranian leaders, such as Rafsanjani and, to a certain extent, Khomeini's successor, Khamenei, realized that Iran's radical policies had led to the country's increasing isolation among its neighbors.

---

[29] Fred Halliday, "Arabian Peninsula Opposition Movements," Middle East Research and Information Project, February 1985.

[30] GlobalSecurity.org, "Shias in Iraq," Web page, last updated on June 22, 2005.

[31] However, this did not mean that the Iranian Revolution was not influential in the Muslim world. It has inspired Islamic fundamentalist movements from Egypt to Pakistan.

From Revolution to Pragmatism—and Back Again?

By 1989, revolutionary turmoil and eight years of constant warfare had left Iran in a precarious position. The Islamic Republic could no longer focus on exporting the revolution at the expense of Iran's national interests, including economic reconstruction. The death of Khomeini also encouraged the ruling elite to approach foreign policy in a more practical and more pragmatic manner. However, competing trends within Iran's strategic culture also led to increased political factionalism.

Iran's ruling elites were not able to reach a consensus regarding either Iran's role in the world or the best approach to strategic and foreign policies. During Rafsanjani's presidency (1989–1997), the technocrats wished to preserve the identity of Iran as an Islamic Republic but also sought a market economy and friendly relations with some neighboring countries. The majority of reformists under the leadership of President Mohammad Khatami (1997–2005), while pledging allegiance to the concept of *velayat-e faqih*, attempted to create both a more inclusive and more democratic political system internally and a dialogue of civilizations with the West.

The elites who have driven Iranian policymaking during the Ahmadinejad administration cling to Iran's earlier revolutionary ideology of *moqavamat*, and they employ this ideological rhetoric in their approach to domestic- and foreign-policy issues. Elites who are more pragmatic argue that Iran's requirements as a functioning nation-state include economic development, regional security, and the confidence of the international community—all of which require a moderate foreign policy. Iran can function as a normal nation-state or a vehicle for revolution, but not necessarily both. Reflecting recent internal disagreements over Khomeini's legacy, Khatami has questioned Iran's policy of exporting the revolution. In a controversial 2008 speech, he asked,

> what did Imam Khomeini mean by exporting the Revolution? Did Imam Khomeini mean that we take up arms, that we blow up places in other nations and we create groups to carry out sabo-

tage in other countries? He was vehemently against such measures and was confronting it [sic].[32]

Khatami and his followers believe that internal reform—not violent revolution—is the key to ensuring the survival and well-being of the Islamic Republic. However, their view of the Islamic Republic as a system capable of fundamental reform seems overoptimistic, since the system is, at its core, an exceptional and revolutionary system established in opposition to the international system. More importantly, Khatami and the reformists have had little power within Iran's political establishment. Moreover, continued instability in the Middle East has only reinforced Iran's revolutionary identity and made economic development and systematic reform more challenging than ever.

The End of Pragmatism?

Iran's strategic outlook is dominated by two principal factors: the perception of the United States as an active threat and a determination to seize for Iran an important and widely recognized role in the Middle East. According to Ahmadinejad,

> the political power of the occupiers [the Americans in Iraq] is collapsing rapidly. Soon, we will see a huge power vacuum in the region. Of course, we are prepared to fill the gap, with the help of neighbors and regional friends like Saudi Arabia, and with the help of the Iraqi nation.[33]

To accomplish what Ahmadinejad envisions, Iran must first weaken, discredit, and, if possible, humiliate the United States while at the same time successfully promoting its own influence and power as an alternative. This ambition has been facilitated by a number of regional trends. Clearly, the elimination of a Sunni- and Baathist-dominated Iraq, which posed one of the most serious threats to Iran's interests, is

---

[32] Parisa Hafezi, "Iran Hardliners Criticize Khatami's 'Insulting' Speech," *Reuters*, May 7, 2008a.

[33] "Ahmadinejad: 'Iran Ready to Fill Iraq Power Vacuum,'" *The Guardian* (London), August 28, 2007.

the foremost event. A future Iraq that is Shi'a-dominated, and perhaps Islamist in nature, could benefit Iranian interests and transform the regional balance of power. Successful Iranian support of Hezbollah in Lebanon and Hamas in Gaza—in addition to the Islamic Republic's backing of multiple Shi'a parties and militias in Iraq—has enhanced Iran's regional influence and provided it strategic depth.[34] Furthermore, in the Iranian view, both the Iraqi insurgency (whether Sunni or Shi'a) and Hezbollah's armed confrontation with Israel in Lebanon in 2006 have exposed the limitations of U.S. and Western military power and have played into Iran's familiar narrative of the effectiveness of *moqavamat*.[35]

These trends have caused great consternation and doubt among U.S.-allied Arab states. Iran has sought to fill a perceived regional security vacuum and undermine the United States and its allies by substituting its own credentials as a regional-security manager. But instead of approaching the Arab states and GCC on the basis of cooperation, Iran is seen to be undermining the regional order, much as it attempted to do during the early years of the revolution. However, Iran's behavior toward the Arab states is much different today than during the revolutionary era. The Islamic Republic has learned that its efforts to export the revolution and Iran's unique of system of government have been mostly unsuccessful. In contrast to its goals in the 1980s, Iran's chief objective now is not to overthrow existing Arab regimes but rather to enhance the Islamic Republic's political, economic, and military influence and power at the expense of the United States and key U.S. allies in the region.

Iran's recent assertiveness is not merely a result of feeling the same type of isolation and sense of siege it experienced during the revolution and the Iran-Iraq War. Rather, it is also due to the fact that Iranian

---

[34] In the past, Iranian leaders characterized their interest in the Palestine issue as a matter of solidarity with oppressed Muslims and a question of justice and conscience. More recently, Palestine has also served as a strategic bulwark, a front line that Iran must support to meet its own defense needs (namely, the need to keep the strategic enemy as distant as possible from Iranian territory).

[35] Arguably, these same issues also demonstrate the limitations of Iranian influence. See discussion later in this chapter and Wehrey, Thaler, et al., 2009, pp. 81–128.

elites and power centers have perceived a changed regional environment that favors Iranian power. Some within Iran's government—particularly Ahmadinejad and his allies—perceive the U.S.-dominated international system to be under great pressure. Whether this perception is realistic or not, these elites also see Iran as having turned a corner and reached a "threshold of a geo-strategic leap."[36] Conservative Iranian commentators point to "the gradual transfer of power and influence from America's camp to Iran's camp" and see the spread of Islamism in the region going hand in hand with "the inclination of regional states to gravitate toward Iran."[37]

The Iranian government's newfound confidence may even convince Iranian pragmatists and outside observers that the regional environment is conducive and even hospitable to the permanent exercise of Iranian influence. However, there are a number of structural problems in the region working against Iran.

Challenges to Iranian Power

In its attempt to assume the leadership of the Muslim Middle East and the Persian Gulf region, Iran is handicapped by its Persian identity and Shi'a persuasion. Furthermore, Iran's increasing influence in Iraq, Syria, Lebanon, and the Palestinian territories has created anxiety among Iran's Arab neighbors. Many of these neighbors view Iran not merely as a source of revolutionary instability but also as a non-Arab hegemonic power intent on dominating the Middle East. Some Iraqi Sunnis, for example, have denounced the "Safavid" influence in their country, and *Safavid* is a term that carries not only sectarian but also distinctly anti-Persian connotations.[38] Even among Iraq's Arab Shi'a,

---

[36] "Iran's Strategy Is to Confront U.S. Unilateralism: Larijani," Mehr News Agency, June 9, 2008.

[37] See, respectively, Payman Tajrishi, Iran Web site, December 15, 2007, in BBC Monitoring, December 16, 2007b; Hanif Ghaffari, Resalat Web site, February 20, 2008, in BBC Monitoring, February 25, 2008b.

[38] Coalition Provisional Authority, *English Translation of Terrorist Musab al Zarqawi Letter Obtained by United States Government in Iraq*, February 2004.

there is wariness toward Iran's perceived interference in Iraqi affairs. In addition, Iran's perceived interference in Lebanon, especially during the May 2008 conflict between the Shi'a group Hezbollah and the Sunni-dominated government of Lebanon, was seen by many Arabs as an attempt by Iran to broaden its regional power.[39] Close relations with Iran can also pose a dilemma for groups, such as Hezbollah, that welcome Iran's patronage but desire a nationalist image.

Thus, Iran's image as a force resisting imperial domination may not withstand geopolitical realities and Arab perceptions. Significant segments of the Iranian population and the elite may still view Iran as a victim of imperialism, but evidence suggests that the region's non-Persian population views Iran as an imperial power. In the Arabic daily *al-Sharq al-Awsat*, respected columnist Mshari al-Thaydi wrote,

> reality exposes an Iranian aggression in the region . . . let's examine all the big Arab portfolios, Lebanon, Palestine, and Iraq. They are being stolen from Arab hands, which have traditionally handled these issues, and turned over to Iranian hands gradually.[40]

In sum, Iran's perception of itself is shaped by a long history of victory and defeat; it sees itself as a once-great power humbled and humiliated by the West, particularly the United States. Furthermore, the Islamic Revolution enhanced Iran's sense of exceptionalism and created a potent mixture of religious ideology and deep-seated nationalism. The Islamic Republic today has the ability to act beyond the confines of the revolution as a nation pursuing nonideological state interests, but its viewpoints and behavior continue to be shaped by Iran's tortured history and identity as a revisionist and revolutionary state.

---

[39] Hugh Sykes, "Hezbollah Is Iran's Lebanese 'Aircraft Carrier,'" Ya Libnan, June 9, 2008.

[40] Mshari al-Thaydi, "Uhadhir an Taqdhi Alihi al-Ama'im [Warning Against the Religious Establishment]," *al-Sharq al-Awsat* (London), July 19, 2007.

CHAPTER THREE

Formal Structures of the Islamic Republic

With Iran's history and strategic culture as our background, we turn now to the structural and institutional factors that influence debates, policymaking, and policy implementation in the Islamic Republic of Iran. The formal context serves as a backdrop to the intense, often brutal political environment that is dominated by factional competition and informal networks, a topic we discuss in Chapter Four. The aim of this chapter is to review Iran's major institutions and the formal powers accorded to them by the constitution.[1] Perhaps most significant is the clear disparity between the official authority of these political organs and the actual authority they exercise. In effect, the daily dynamics of Iran's political system do not accurately adhere to the formal structures described in the country's constitution. There are at least three main reasons for the differences between prescribed and exercised authorities.

First, an office's title is only as meaningful as the person who holds it. In other words, the relative influence an institution has in policymaking depends not only on the constitutional powers ascribed to it but also on the influence of the personality in charge. This is a topic we discuss in detail in Chapter Four.

Second, the duality of theocracy and republicanism in the Iranian system complicates matters further. The Iranian constitution empowers unelected, appointed institutions to challenge, undermine,

---

[1] For a translation of the constitution, see Axel Tschentscher, ed., *Iran—Constitution [A Translation of the Constitution of the Islamic Republic of Iran]*, International Constitutional Law, last updated in 1995.

and override the decisions made by the elected president (and his cabinet) and parliament.[2] Unelected bodies, such as the Guardian Council, also vet candidates for elected office and disqualify candidates deemed unworthy based on a perceived lack of their adherence to revolutionary and Islamic values. The dominance of these unelected bodies thereby circumscribes the authorities of the legislative and executive branches and suppresses freedom of speech, assembly, due process, and other democratic principles.

Finally, the establishment and empowerment of multiple institutions that perform identical or similar functions—and therefore compete with each other for resources and status—has generated a diffuse and complicated political system. In theory, this multifarious, redundant design prevents any one center of power from gaining undue influence over the entire system and ensures the overall survival and security of the regime and the central position of the Supreme Leader. In reality, however, it results in friction and competition, even among state elites at the highest levels.[3] For instance, the executive branch shares some of its policymaking responsibilities with the Supreme Leader; the legislative branch is comprised of two separate institutions, the Guardian Council and the Majles (the Iranian parliament), and the Guardian Council has direct authority over the Majles' elections and legislation; and the armed forces are bifurcated between a regular army (the Artesh) and the Islamic Revolutionary Guard Corps (IRGC). Iran's leadership has made some effort to mitigate these overlapping authorities; for example, the Expediency Council was created to break a recurring logjam between the Majles and the Guardian Council. Additionally, in an effort to streamline the executive, the position of the prime minister was eliminated in 1989, and the president was put directly in charge of administrative and budgetary matters.[4] These constitutional changes, however, do not seem to have liberated the system of func-

---

[2]   Mehdi Moslem, *Factional Politics in Post-Khomeini Iran*, Syracuse, N.Y.: Syracuse University Press, 2002, p. 11.

[3]   Mehran Kamrava, "Iranian National-Security Debates: Factionalism and Lost Opportunities," *Middle East Policy*, Vol. 14, No. 2, Summer 2007, pp. 85–87.

[4]   Tschentscher, 1995, Article 126.

tionally similar institutions in competition with each other, and stasis and deadlock still frequently occur.

Thus, Iran's constitution and formal political institutions do not fully shape or describe the entirety of the country's political system. However, it is important to understand these formal institutional structures as a playing field upon which other, less-formal parts of the system interact. Figure 3.1 outlines the hierarchy of Iran's political institutions

Figure 3.1
Distribution of Power in the Constitution

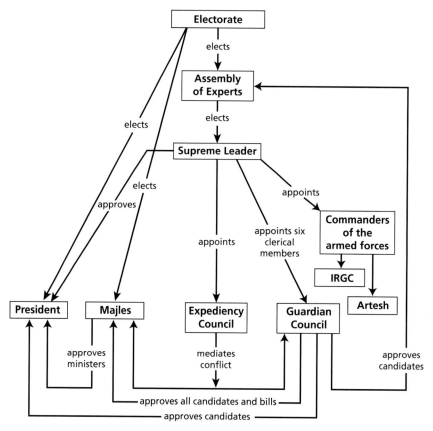

SOURCE: Adapted from Mehran Kamrava and Houchang Hassan-Yari, "Suspended Equilibrium in Iran's Political System," *The Muslim World*, Vol. 94, October 2004, p. 506.

and their relationships with each other. As one can see, the Supreme Leader sits at the top and center of Iran's political system and has direct and indirect reach into all other government organs. This diagram is a starting point for the rest of the chapter, which describes in greater detail Iran's principle governmental organizations, their formal and informal powers, and their relationships with other institutions.

The Supreme Leader

The Supreme Leader, who is appointed for life by the Assembly of Experts, sits at the apex of Iran's formal power structure. His authority is derived from Khomeini's principle of *velayat-e faqih*, which was codified in the constitution after the Islamic Revolution.[5] The constitution gives the Supreme Leader the authority to delineate "the general policies of the Islamic Republic" and to supervise "the proper execution of the general policies of the system."[6] The Supreme Leader ratifies the electorate's choice of president and directly appoints senior state officials. He is commander in chief of the armed forces and appoints the commanders of the IRGC, the Artesh, and the Joint Staff of the Armed Forces. He appoints the heads of the judiciary and of Islamic Republic of Iran Broadcasting, and he appoints and dismisses the clerical jurists of the Guardian Council. The Supreme Leader also appoints numerous so-called special representatives throughout the government—and in various religious and cultural institutions—who serve as his eyes and ears and enable him to exert influence and control throughout the political system and ensure that his policies are implemented by various agencies. These representatives include the directors of cultural bureaus based in Iran's worldwide embassies, allowing the Supreme Leader to shape Iran's foreign policy independently. The Supreme Leader also appoints all Friday-prayer leaders, who disseminate his political message and ideology to the larger population.

---

[5]   Under this principle, the Supreme Leader is the ultimate authority and the earthly trustee of the Shi'a "Hidden Imam" until the latter's reappearance on the Day of Judgment.

[6]   Tschentscher, 1995, Article 110.

The Supreme Leader also appoints the directors of Iran's *bonyads* [foundations], which function as independent economic entities and patronage networks unaccountable to the state.[7] Finally, the Supreme Leader relies on his own powerful secretariat, the Office of the Supreme Leader [*daftar-e maqam-e mo'azzam-e rahbari*] for advice in all fields, including defense and foreign policy.[8]

Thus, the Supreme Leader's constitutional powers are unparalleled in Iran's political system. In Chapter Four, we discuss the considerable informal powers that the Supreme Leader wields.

The President

The president, the formal head of the executive branch, is ostensibly the second highest-ranking official, next in line after the Supreme Leader.[9] The president is elected by popular vote every four years for up to two terms, although the Guardian Council must approve all presidential candidates.[10] As the chief executive, the president is responsible for the day-to-day administration of the country and for enforcing the constitution.[11] Additionally, he heads the Council of Ministers and chairs the Supreme National Security Council (SNSC), implements laws passed by the Majles or by referenda, signs international treaties and agreements, takes responsibility for state budgetary and administrative matters, accepts the credentials of foreign ambassadors and signs the credentials of Iran's ambassadors, and nominates and terminates the tenure of cabinet ministers.

---

[7]   See Wilfried Buchta, *Who Rules Iran? The Structure of Power in the Islamic Republic*, Washington, D.C.: The Washington Institute for Near East Policy and the Konrad Adenauer Stiftung, 2000, pp. 47–52.

[8]   In early 2007, the Supreme Leader sent his secretariat chief of staff, Mohammad Golpayegani, to Moscow to discuss Iranian-Russian relations.

[9]   However, it is Rafsanjani who is referred to as both Iran's "second most *powerful* man" and the only individual in the Islamic Republic who can be considered a potential political rival to Khamenei (Sadjadpour, 2008, p. 27).

[10]   Tschentscher, 1995, Article 99, Article 114.

[11]   Tschentscher, 1995, Article 113.

Although the president's authority is limited constitutionally in deference to that of the Supreme Leader, the administrations of Khatami (1997–2005) and Ahmadinejad (2005–present) have tested the bounds of presidential authority. Khatami attempted to inject greater openness in to Iranian political life and society in general. The Supreme Leader was wary of Khatami throughout his presidency, a reflection of the deeper tensions between religious rule and the reformist aspirations of Khatami and many of his Iranian followers. The historical tension between the office of the Supreme Leader and the presidency increased significantly during Khatami's term in office. This tension was evident in the 2004 Majles elections, which saw the disqualification of many reformist candidates by the conservative Guardian Council, whose members are appointed (directly and indirectly, as discussed in a later section) by the Supreme Leader.[12] In contrast, Ahmadinejad, who has sought to shape Iran's foreign and nuclear policies, has a closer relationship with the Supreme Leader. Khamenei favors Ahmadinejad, who is more conservative than Khatami, and expressed his support for Ahmadinejad in the 2005 presidential election, the 2008 parliamentary elections, and the most recent presidential election. Conversely, Khatami's efforts at reform were greatly hindered by Khamenei's opposition to the president's agenda. The differences between the Khatami and Ahmadinejad cases highlight the importance of personal ties and worldview in the relationship between the president and the Supreme Leader in terms of the ability of a president to pursue his own agenda.

Further, although the constitutional authority of the Supreme Leader certainly dwarfs that of the president, the two offices share some responsibilities. This has led to institutional competition and, at times, strategic stalemate. For instance, although the Supreme Leader commands the armed forces and offers overall strategic guidance, the president may drive formulation and implementation of specific domestic and foreign policies. And, although the Supreme Leader is the ultimate decisionmaker, the president can frame a foreign or domestic issue in such a way that the Supreme Leader has little choice but to support the president's position. A good example of this is Ahmadinejad's assertion

---

[12] BBC News, "Iran: Who Holds the Power?" Web page, undated.

that Iran's nuclear program is a national right. Painting the issue as a fundamental matter of sovereignty and independence makes it difficult for anyone (including Khamenei) to compromise with the international community. In recent years, Khamenei has sought to distance himself from Khatami's diplomatic strategy vis-à-vis the West (a strategy over which Khamenei himself ostensibly presided).

The president has the authority to choose the Council of Ministers (his cabinet), but the Majles must first approve the candidates and has the right to impeach ministers it judges to have performed unsatisfactorily. For example, the Majles rejected several of Ahmadinejad's first-term nominees for the key post of oil minister, a huge embarrassment for the president and a sign of the independence and power of the legislative branch.[13] In another area of potential overlapping authorities and conflict, the Council of Ministers and the Office of the Supreme Leader both concentrate heavily on security- and foreign-policy issues, thereby rivaling each other's efforts.

The Majles

The 290-member Majles has the constitutional authority to review and approve government budgets, propose bills, ratify international treaties, and review the performance of the president and his ministers.[14] When the Majles passes a law that is controversial and whose adherence to Islamic law and the constitution is questionable, the law becomes subject to the Guardian Council's intervention and, in case of conflict between the two bodies, to the decisions of the Expediency Council (an organization described in a later section).

The Majles speaker has the ability to define the relationship between the Majles and the presidency. Gholam-Ali Haddad-Adel, a former Majles speaker and a relative of Khamenei by marriage, was largely supportive of the Ahmadinejad administration until the last

---

[13] "Iranian MPs Reject Oil Minister," BBC News, November 23, 2005.

[14] See Tschentscher, 1995, Articles 71–90. The number of deputies was increased from 270 in the 2000 elections.

few months of his speakership. Larijani, the current speaker, has been much more critical of Ahmadinejad—particularly in the foreign- and nuclear-policy realms—and has insinuated that the Majles may oppose some of Ahmadinejad's policies.[15]

However, the speaker's disagreements with the president over foreign policy do not change the fact that the Majles deputies are overwhelmingly concerned with local as opposed to national (let alone foreign) affairs. Perhaps only one-quarter of the 290 deputies are interested in broader issues.[16] In addition, the Supreme Leader has the last word on all policies because all Majles candidates are vetted by the Guardian Council to ensure loyalty to the regime and *velayat-e faqih.*

The Assembly of Experts

The Assembly of Experts is a body comprised of 86 senior clerics, each vetted by the Guardian Council and elected by popular vote to eight-year terms. Headed since 2007 by Rafsanjani, the assembly's primary task is to appoint and "supervise" the Supreme Leader, and for this reason all of its members are required to be experts in *fiqh* [Islamic jurisprudence].[17] As expected, most members of the assembly are religiously and socially conservative. The assembly's meetings are not based on a predetermined schedule, and its deliberations remain closed and secretive: The assembly has not published a single public report. Members gather at least once a year for a two-day meeting, usually in Tehran, and can hold consultative meetings when crisis situations demand them. The body is considered an essential pillar of Iran's formal political system because it has the authority to dismiss the Supreme Leader if he no longer meets the criteria set by the constitution or is unable to execute his duties satisfactorily.

---

[15] See, for example, Kamal Nazer Yasin, "Iran: Conservatives Trying to Get President Ahmadinejad to Moderate Behavior," EurasiaNet.org, June 10, 2008.

[16] Author discussion with a consultant based in Tehran, March 18, 2008. Most of the deputies in this subset come from more-urban areas.

[17] Tschentscher, 1995, Articles 107 and 111.

Despite its constitutional importance, traditionally, the Assembly of Experts has not been a very active player in Iranian political discourse. In appointing Khamenei as Khomeini's successor in 1989, its role was more to serve as a rubber stamp on Khomeini's wishes rather than to act as an independent decisionmaker.

The Guardian Council

The Guardian Council, an appointed body with a traditionally conservative outlook, consists of 12 jurists, six of whom are *foqaha* [Islamic jurisprudents] selected for six-year terms by the Supreme Leader. The remaining members are nonclerical jurists appointed by the Majles at the recommendation of the head of the judiciary, who is in turn appointed by the Supreme Leader.[18] Ayatollah Ahmad Jannati has been the head of the council since 1996. Under Article 98 of the constitution, the council has the authority to interpret the constitution and can block legislation that it deems un-Islamic or in violation of the constitution. If the laws do not pass such examination, the council refers them back to the Majles for revision. A council ruling reached by three-fourths of the members assumes the same validity as the constitution itself.[19]

Article 99 of the constitution grants the council supreme oversight over all public referenda and the elections for the Majles, the Assembly of Experts, and the presidency. In effect, the council has the power to shape the elections in such a way that the electorate must choose from a list of vetted candidates who are compatible with the council's (and the Supreme Leader's) outlook. Based on an examination of candidates' Islamic convictions and loyalty to the regime, the council decides whether these parliamentary and presidential aspirants are qualified to run for office.[20] Indeed, there has been much controversy over the Guardian Council's use of its assigned powers, particularly its

---

[18] Tschentscher, 1995, Article 91.

[19] Tschentscher, 1995, Article 91.

[20] Buchta, 2000, p. 59.

right to exercise *nizarate-e estisvabi* [approbatory supervision], which allows it to disqualify candidates who do not meet its standards.[21] As one scholar argues, this supervisory power, which gives the council's six clerical members extensive oversight over Iranian elections, is one of the main obstacles to the development of a true democracy in Iran.[22] Reformist attempts to reduce the council's vetting powers have proved unsuccessful, exemplified by the disqualification of more than 1,000 candidates (including all of the female candidates) prior to the 2005 presidential elections.[23] In addition, the Guardian Council was viewed by reformists and even many conservatives as having favored Ahmadinejad during the 2009 presidential-election dispute. The Guardian Council's predisposition to extend its hand and influence elections reaffirms the duality of theocracy and republicanism in Iran—the former often dominates the latter.

The Expediency Council

Khomeini decreed the creation of the Expediency Council in February 1988, envisioning it as a body that would break deadlocks between the Guardian Council and the Majles and advise the Supreme Leader on his constitutional responsibilities.[24] Since 1989, the Supreme Leader has relied on the Expediency Council for advice on domestic policies. Currently headed by Rafsanjani, the council is composed of some 35–40 permanent and temporary members representing many major government factions (factions are discussed at length in Chapter Four), the heads of the three branches of government, and the clerical mem-

---

[21] The meaning of the Assembly of Experts' term *approbatory supervision* is still open to debate today.

[22] Abbas William Samii, "Iran's Guardians Council as an Obstacle to Democracy," *Middle East Journal*, Vol. 55, No. 4, Autumn 2001.

[23] BBC News, undated.

[24] Tschentscher, 1995, Article 112. Here the translation says "Exigency Council," but we prefer "Expediency," which is the more broadly applied English term.

bers of the Guardian Council.[25] The Supreme Leader appoints permanent members for five-year terms; the temporary members who represent government ministries and the Majles are selected when issues under the council's jurisdiction come before it. The Supreme Leader can ask the council to explore any issue he deems necessary. Following the election of Ahmadinejad in 2005, Khamenei granted the Expediency Council undefined "supervisory authority" over the three branches of government, presumably including foreign affairs; some have speculated that this was done to limit Ahmadinejad's authority.[26]

The Judiciary

The 1979 constitution made the judiciary an independent power and charged it with the enforcement of Islamic law. Another formal purpose of the body is to nominate the six lay members to the Guardian Council. The head of the judiciary (as of August 2009, Ayatollah Sadeq Ardeshir Larijani, a brother of Ali Larijani), serves a five-year term and is appointed by and reports directly to the Supreme Leader. This allows the Supreme Leader to shape the makeup of the lay section of the Guardian Council, and it strengthens his influence over the council's vetting of candidates. The head of the judiciary works with the minister of justice, who is chosen by the president and is responsible for all matters concerning the relationship between the judiciary and the executive and legislative branches.[27] Importantly, the fact that the president chooses the minister of justice and the Supreme Leader chooses the head of the judiciary illustrates yet another area of overlapping formal authority in the system and a potential source of friction between the president and Supreme Leader.

---

[25] Abbas Maleki, "Decision-Making in Iran's Foreign Policy: A Heuristic Approach," *Journal of Social Affairs*, Vol. 19, No. 73, Spring 2002, pp. 39–40.

[26] See Walter Posch, *Iran's Domestic Politics—The "Circles of Influence:" Ahmadinejad's Enigmatic Networks*, IESUE/COPS/INF 0521, Paris: European Union Institute for Security Studies, October 19, 2005b, pp. 20–21.

[27] Tschentscher, 1995, Article 160.

The Supreme National Security Council

Chaired by the president, the SNSC is the Islamic Republic's key national defense and security body. Article 176 of the constitution states that the SNSC's responsibilities include determining "the defense and national security policies within the framework of general policies determined by the Leader"; coordinating "activities in the areas relating to politics, intelligence, social, cultural, and economic fields in regard to general defense and security policies"; and exploiting "materialistic and intellectual resources of the country for facing the internal and external threats."[28] The SNSC evolved in 1988 from the earlier Supreme Defense Council and was mandated by the revised constitution of 1989. In addition to the president, formal members of the SNCS include the ministers of foreign affairs, interior, and intelligence; the chiefs of the IRGC and Artesh; the heads of the legislative and judicial branches; and two personal representatives of the Supreme Leader.

The SNSC's membership is fluid, and the identity of participants in policy discussions is determined by the issue under consideration. In the area of Iran's nuclear program, it appears that Rafsanjani, Larijani (the previous chief nuclear negotiator and the previous SNSC secretary), the head of the Atomic Energy Organization of Iran, and Ali Akbar Velayati and Kamal Kharrazi (special advisors to the Supreme Leader on foreign affairs) are involved. According to Larijani, the secretary of the SNSC spends "about 20 percent of his time" on nuclear issues.[29] It appears that decisions made in the SNSC, once approved by the Supreme Leader, become consensus decisions. This implies that further discussion is proscribed, and the press is advised accordingly. Under Ahmadinejad, the SNSC has recently gone further than just warning the press of the limits of discussion: It has provided guide-

---

[28] Tschentscher, 1995, Article 176. For background on the SNSC, see Hasan Rowhani, interview with *Tehran-e Emrooz* (Tehran), BBC Monitoring, December 15, 2006; Wilfried Buchta, *Iran's Security Sector: An Overview*, Geneva Center for the Democratic Control of Armed Forces, Working Paper No. 146, August 2004, pp. 17–18.

[29] Ali Larijani, "Interview," *Hamshahri Newspaper* (Tehran), November 10, 2007, in BBC Monitoring, December 13, 2007e.

lines (or official spin) on to how the Iranian press is to report and depict the "nuclear story."[30]

The Strategic Council for Foreign Relations

Although it is not a constitutionally mandated body, the Strategic Council for Foreign Relations (SCFR) is an important advisory council to the Supreme Leader. Khamenei established the SCFR after Ahmadinejad had been in office one year, possibly to maintain access to seasoned foreign-policy advice in light of the Ahmadinejad team's inexperience. Kharrazi, foreign minister during Khatami's administration, heads the council. Other members include Velayati, a long-time foreign-policy advisor to the Supreme Leader and foreign minister under the Rafsanjani administration, and Ali Shamkhani, former defense minister under Khatami.[31]

Iran's Security Forces[32]

Like Iran's political system, Iran's security institutions are marked by overlapping, redundant responsibilities that at times bring organizations into competition over funding, equipment, and influence. Iran's armed forces are divided into two branches, the IRGC and the Artesh, a division that reflects the revolutionary regime's early concerns about the loyalty of the Shah's armed forces.

Both the IRGC and the Artesh field separate armies, navies, and air forces, and both play roles in the defense of Iran against external aggression. The Artesh is the larger and more conventional of the two branches. In addition to defending Iran against external threats, the IRGC pursues missions related to internal security and regime survival

---

[30] See "New SCNS Guidelines for Press," Iran Press Service, March 6, 2008.

[31] Abbas William Samii, "Iran: New Foreign Policy Council Could Curtail Ahmadinejad's Power," Radio Free Europe/Radio Liberty, June 29, 2006a.

[32] For a comprehensive discussion of the objectives, structures, doctrine, and capabilities of Iran's security forces, see Wehrey, Thaler, et al., 2009, pp. 39–80.

(even more so since the 2009 election), where its roles overlap with those of the Law Enforcement Forces (LEF) and the Ministry of Intelligence and Security (MOIS). Importantly, the IRGC controls most of Iran's missile forces and is heavily involved in Iran's nuclear program. As the discussion in Chapter Four demonstrates, the IRGC has gained political and economic power during the present decade and likely played a major role in Ahmadinejad's declared electoral "victory" in June 2009. The IRGC–Qods Force, other elements of the IRGC, and the MOIS all play a role in collecting intelligence, intimidating dissidents, and nurturing pro-Iranian proxies in foreign nations. Finally, the MOIS shares its domestic-security responsibilities with other institutions: the Basij militia, the LEF, and some vigilante or pressure groups often associated with prominent ultraconservative clerics.

Used by the IRGC and the regime as a vehicle for indoctrinating the populace, the Basij Resistance Force is a popular reserve force headed by an IRGC principal with an active strength of perhaps 300,000 and a claimed mobilization capacity of 5 million. The Basij are present in virtually all sectors of Iranian society: There are specially organized Basij units for university students, local tribes and villages, factory workers, and so forth.[33]

The LEF, which is subordinate to the Ministry of Interior, has diverse responsibilities, including counternarcotics, riot control, border protection, enforcing morality laws, and anticorruption.[34] In some ways the LEF, which employs roughly 120,000 personnel, resembles European-style gendarmeries because it functions much like a national police force responsible for fighting organized and petty crime. The LEF should also be viewed as an internal-security force ready to crush dissent, much like the IRGC and the Basij. However, it has at times come into conflict with vigilante groups, such as Ansar-e Hezbollah.[35]

---

[33] Anthony H. Cordesman and Martin Kleiber, *Iran's Military Forces and Warfighting Capabilities: The Threat in the Northern Gulf,* Washington, D.C.: Center for Strategic and International Studies, 2007, pp. 12–13; Byman et al., 2001, pp. 38–39; "The Basij Resistance Force," in *How They Fight: Armies of the World,* National Ground Intelligence Center, NGIC-1122-0204-98, 1998.

[34] Buchta, 2004, pp. 11–12.

[35] Wehrey, Green, et al., 2009, p. 11.

Concluding Remarks: Formal Structures

Despite constitutional requisites designed to build consensus and separate powers, the Iranian political system remains bifurcated, with political authority traditionally split between *velayat-e faqih* (embodied in the person of a religious Supreme Leader) on the one hand and a popularly elected executive and legislature on the other (although the ongoing militarization of Iranian politics under the Revolutionary Guards undermines the viability of elections). The unelected theocratic institutions tend to dominate the elected republican ones, and many of Iran's institutions have overlapping missions. Even the institutions created to mitigate such overlap, such as the Expediency Council, have themselves fallen victim to the system and become key participants in factional conflict. This helps insulate the regime against internal threats to stability and its own survival. This same competition, however, introduces excessive complexity and paralysis into the system—features that are further compounded by multiple informal power centers. Often more influential than official institutions and structures, these informal networks enable network members to wield power and influence in the system.

The aim of the next chapter is to describe this complex undercurrent of informal networks of patronage and political mobilization that dominates Iran's political landscape.

CHAPTER FOUR

Factionalism and the Primacy of Informal Networks

In the United States, people become rich and then go into politics;
in Iran, people go into politics to become rich.

—Iranian political aphorism

After leading the revolution that brought down the Shah in the spring
of 1979, Khomeini led the struggle of transforming Iran into an Islamic
Republic while consolidating his own power among the various revolutionary groups. The process of building a new form of government was
not straightforward, and there were conflicting views among revolutionaries from across the political spectrum about the appropriate nature
of the new regime. But Khomeini and the Islamist revolutionaries who
supported him were also keenly aware of and motivated by Iran's long
and bitter experiences with foreign (especially U.S. and British) domination of the country's internal politics.[1] In the end, an impenetrable
and complicated system of overlapping authorities emerged.

The result is what has been termed a state of "suspended
equilibrium"[2] that has taken the shape of a peculiarly Iranian style of
checks and balances, ensuring that no one faction becomes so dominant as to challenge the Supreme Leader or gain ultimate power within
the system. However, there are indications (which we discuss in Chapter Five) that this equilibrium may erode over the next few years as

---

[1] Of particular note are the U.S. Central Intelligence Agency–orchestrated overthrow of
Mossadegh in 1953 and the close relationship between the Shah and the United States until
the 1979 revolution.

[2] See Mehran Kamrava and Houchang Hassan-Yari, "Suspended Equilibrium in Iran's
Political System," *The Muslim World*, Vol. 94, October 2004.

Iran's conservative elites, including those of the IRGC, expand their dominance of state institutions and resources.

The overlapping and factional nature of the Iranian regime is a source of its very stability and survival. But it is also a recipe for gridlock because the multiple power centers and factions tend to neutralize one another. Paralysis is normal, innovation and strategic decisionmaking abnormal; the lowest common denominator often rules. A characteristic of such a rigid and immobile system is the prevalence of *negative power*: The power to block is widely dispersed, but the power to initiate is scarce. The result is that the system rarely begets strategic decisions without first identifying a broadly recognized threat to the survival of the regime. Fear of change is reflected in the system's basic incrementalism. Change threatens control over the system and is therefore denied or avoided. Crisis is the primary means of unblocking the system and pushing it in a particular direction (although politics may evolve over time in certain directions). Yet Iran does function. Often, consensus and decisiveness among the political elite are issue-dependent; for example, it is possible to identify greater consensus over the nuclear program than over either Iran's relations with the Arab world or the management of Iran's economy (see Chapter Five).

Thus, it is important to view Iran through the lens of the bonds of patronage and loyalty that exist among various individuals and groups and not simply through the lens of the regime's ideological and formal, or bureaucratic, characteristics. In this chapter, we seek to provide insight into the factional relationships and informal networks that often drive Iranian leadership dynamics and elite behavior. First, the chapter characterizes some of the most-important informal networks in the Islamic Republic and identifies trends in these networks since the 1979 revolution. We describe the Iranian system as a web of key personalities, the informal networks upon which these personalities draw, and the institutions these personalities dominate. Our research indicates a pattern in which one type of network attains primacy in Iranian political and economic life for about a decade and is then eclipsed by another, although less-dominant networks remain influential. Second, we explore what can be described as *supernetworks*—political factions that bring together multiple types of networks around a common worldview or stance on a key policy issue. Factional competition is a staple of political life in the Islamic Republic. Debates regarding Iran's foreign, economic, and social policies often reflect factional maneuvering for domestic power and influence as much as disagreement over the policies themselves. Policy issues are at times of secondary concern, although, to the outside world, policy debates may be the most visible manifestations of domestic competition for influence (and often are misconstrued in the West as pronouncements of government policy).[3] Finally, we offer some concluding remarks.

The System: A Web of Personalities, Networks, and Institutions

In his opening remarks at a conference on Iran in February 2008 in Washington, D.C., one observer of the Iranian regime opined that if Rafsanjani, who is considered a consummate political player in the Islamic Republic, were to be brought to the United States and pressed to reveal his voluminous knowledge about the Iranian elites and the networks that bind them, even *he* could not fully describe them.[4] On the other hand, Rafsanjani could describe how he has survived politically for the past quarter century, how he gets things done, and how he gains or maintains power and influence within the Iranian system. It would be virtually impossible to construct a precise organizational chart detailing all the informal networks and their interrelationships— especially difficult from afar, but challenging even from Tehran. Rather than attempt such an undertaking, we seek to broadly characterize and prioritize the networks, describe their effects on the Iranian polity, and identify trends in their evolution. Our overall goal is to provide insight into the character of the Iranian system, not to detail its constituent pieces and interrelationships.

---

[3] How these debates have affected policymaking is the focus of Chapter Five.

[4] Kenneth Pollack of the Brookings Institution opined that "this is a very, very difficult regime to understand . . . . It is very hard even for insiders to fully grasp all of its complexities, let alone to be able to predict what this regime is likely to do next" (Kenneth Pollack, comments at "Iran on the Horizon, Panel II: Iran and the Gulf," Middle East Institute Conference Series, Middle East Institute, Washington, D.C., February 1, 2008).

So, how can one describe the Iranian system? Broadly speaking, the system is a composite of key personalities, their informal networks and relationships with other individuals and power centers (all of which converge over common interests in the form of political factions), and the institutions with which they are associated. Figure 4.1 provides a visual depiction of this system, and, in the following pages, we describe each element in detail.

A number of key personalities (including, first and foremost, Khamenei) have dominated the political elite in Iran, largely since the 1979 revolution and certainly since Khomeini's death a decade later. These personalities draw upon multiple networks of various commonalities—interleaved family, experiential, clerical, political, financial, and other relationships and interests which themselves may constitute power centers—that serve as levers of patronage, mobilization, and dissent. Multiple personalities and networks that share common worldviews and policy positions join forces in political factions. Individuals use their positions in institutions to acquire financial wealth and become sources of patronage, thereby empowering their own families, allies, and networks. The more powerful, influential, and well-connected the individual or individuals leading an institution are, the greater the weight that institution gains in policymaking and implementation within Iran. Finally, the Supreme Leader himself is at the center of this complex web of interrelationships, and often it is proximity to and having the confidence of the Supreme Leader that enables other personalities, networks, and power centers to gain and maintain positions of influence in the system. In sum, it is the combination of key personalities, networks based on a number of commonalities, and institutions—not any one of these elements alone—that defines the political system of the Islamic Republic.

These are, of course, generalizations, and we provide supporting examples below. However, it should be noted that informal networks with powerful patrons are not new to Iran: They predate the Islamic Republic by decades or centuries. Moreover, these networks transcend Iran's borders, especially in the cases of family and religious ties.

Renowned Iran scholar James A. Bill, writing in 1972, when Iran was still a monarchy under the Shah, noted that Iran's system was

Figure 4.1
Examples of Personalities, Informal Networks, Power Centers, Institutions, and Factions in the Iranian System

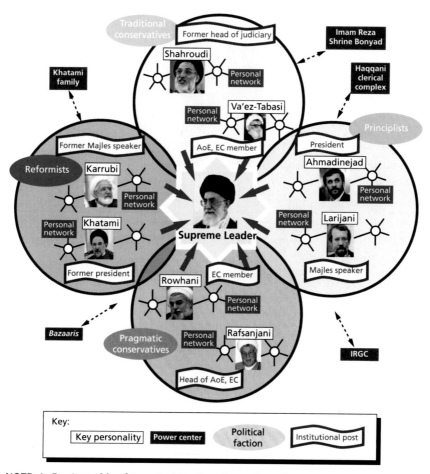

NOTE: AoE = Assembly of Experts; EC = Expediency Council.

RAND *MG878-4.1*

"multi-layered and honey-combed with complex networks of informal groups," with the Shah at the center of many such networks.[5] Observ-

---

[5]   Quoted in Abbas William Samii, "It's Who You Know—Informal Networks in Iran," unpublished paper, undated [c. 2004], pp. 33–35. Samii wrote the paper while he was the regional analysis coordinator for Southwest Asia at Radio Free Europe/Radio Liberty.

ing that "the exercise of power in Iran has been marked by the fact that it has been largely done informally and very personally," Bill noted that Iranian elites engaged in systemic conflict with their peers "to gain greater favor with the Shah and at the same time to capture more control in the Iranian economic arena."[6]

Given the complex and cumbersome formal bureaucracy under the Shah (a state of affairs that continued under the Islamic Republic, but with more democratic trappings), many among the elite preferred to use their relationships with influential individuals and groups to get things done and gain common benefits. In 1959, Richard Gable reported that Iranians had learned "to circumvent formal government procedures. . . . Family and personal influence have come to be so important that there is a common feeling that nothing can be accomplished through regular channels."[7] For example, middle- and upper-class Iranians belonged to one or more *dowreh* [circle] groups, which were gatherings of a dozen or so people who met once a week to discuss and pursue matters of common interest. These groups shared members with others, and newly formed networks became informal conduits for action and rapid communication. Individuals who carried information and demands between *dowrehs* earned a level of influence that was independent of their official positions. Such networks at times encompassed or overlapped *bazaari* [mercantile], religious, and other institutions.[8] According to Bill,

> it is the *dowreh* system and informal net of groups which has been the scene of important business, political or otherwise. The *dowreh* system can be considered both as a kind of web-system itself and as the vehicle through which the rivalries and conflicts pass. The important bargaining, negotiating, and decision making takes place at the card table, in the garden, or on a hike.[9]

---

[6]   James A. Bill, *The Politics of Iran: Groups, Classes and Modernization*, Columbus, Ohio: Charles E. Merrill Publishing Company, 1972, pp. 41, 45.

[7]   Richard W. Gable, "Culture and Administration in Iran," *Middle East Journal*, Vol. 13, No. 4, Fall 1959, p. 411.

[8]   Samii, undated [c. 2004], pp. 33–35.

[9]   Bill, 1972, p. 46.

Thus, the elite in Iranian society gain access and influence through a web of informal relationships that predate the 1979 revolution. Our discussions in later sections provide examples of networks based on clerical background, familial ties, shared military experience, and other common interests. However, in the Islamic Republic, successful networks or groups—i.e., those whose members enjoy significant access to power and the resources of the state—are associated with major individual benefactors with proximity to the Supreme Leader, the highest authority in the land.

A Men's Club of Key Personalities

A small number of prominent individuals have maintained key leadership roles in Iran's political, religious, or economic spheres for the last two-and-a-half decades. Their names—Khamenei, Rafsanjani, Jannati, Larijani, and Mesbah-Yazdi—are often quite familiar to most Western observers, although some are not. They have persevered because of their cohesion on the philosophical and ideological concept of a theocratic regime under *velayat-e faqih*. They survived the Iran-Iraq War, the leftist assassination campaign in the 1980s, and the reformist challenge in the 1990s. One scholar on Iran termed this august group a "men's club" to capture the group's exclusivity and consistent composition (and, of course, the gender of its members).[10] The members of this club do not retire voluntarily from politics; only forcible exclusion or death remove these individuals from the scene. In fact, they "remake" themselves in order to retain positions of influence when adversity requires adaptation. A prime example of this phenomenon is Rafsanjani, who, after being unable even to get elected to the Majles in 2004, almost won the presidency in 2005 and now holds some of the most-important positions in Iran, including the chairmanships of the Assembly of Experts and the Expediency Council.

These elite individuals are not all-powerful; rather, they act like gatekeepers, carefully vetting new prospects for entry into the elite

---

[10] Author telephone discussion with an Iran scholar, March 4, 2008.

through elections or appointments.[11] As of 2009, many of the members of the men's club are in their 60s and 70s, and they are increasingly being challenged by a new generation of leaders—including Ahmadinejad—whom they seek alternately to groom and to control. This wrangling has at times led these elites to support multiple, even competing groups. The new generation is less tied to the clerics who form the base of the theocracy, and many are veterans of the Revolutionary Guards and the Iran-Iraq War. Moreover, the new generation of clerics will, in the future, seek to take the reins of theocratic government as their aging mentors pass from the scene.

Despite the challenges presented by the new generation—the future members of a new men's club—the old guard remains vigorous and predominant in Iranian government and society. Chief among these personalities is Khamenei, who, as Supreme Leader, seeks to ensure above all the survival of the regime and the perpetuation of both the status quo and the Iranian system of checks and balances. The Supreme Leader is, therefore, the ultimate gatekeeper.

The Supreme Leader: A Dominant Personality, but His Power Is Not Limitless

Khamenei has been perceived as indecisive, lacking charisma, and bearing unremarkable religious credentials—especially in contrast to the father of the Islamic Revolution, Khomeini. Yet, despite these perceived weaknesses, Khamenei remains the central figure in the Islamic Republic. Although he does not appear to make major decisions of national import without reference to the opinions of the elite, no major decision can be made without his consent. Moreover, proximity to the Supreme Leader is an important lever of influence for the other individuals in the ruling elite, who advance their positions by gaining and maintaining the Supreme Leader's confidence.

A disciple of Khomeini, Khamenei was a minister of defense, supervisor of the Revolutionary Guards, and Friday-prayer leader in Tehran during the early days after the revolution. In 1981, he was elected president of Iran—during this period, a post with limited constitu-

---

[11] Author telephone discussions with multiple Iran scholars, February and March 2008.

tional authority—and served for two terms until his mentor's death in 1989. A unique confluence of events led to the selection of Khamenei to take Khomeini's place as Supreme Leader. In the 1980s, Khomeini had a falling out with his designated successor, Ayatollah Hossein Ali Montazeri, and was reportedly unhappy with the other senior Iranian clerics who were potential replacements. The Islamic Republic's original constitution called for an *ayatollah al-ozma* [grand ayatollah] to be Supreme Leader, but Khomeini decided three months before his death in 1989 to broaden the pool of candidates by revising the constitution. The revisions require only that the Supreme Leader be an expert in Islamic jurisprudence, a "just and pious person who is fully aware of the circumstances of his age," and an individual who is "possessed of administrative ability."[12] This opened the door for Khamenei—who was close to Khomeini but possessed a less-advanced religious education, which earned him only the middle ranking of *hojjatoleslam* [authority on Islam]—to be eligible for the position. In addition, Rafsanjani, the speaker of the Majles at the time and a strong ally of Khamenei, lobbied hard following Khomeini's death to have Khamenei selected by the Assembly of Experts to be Supreme Leader. Khamenei was seen as agreeable to the country's political elites, although the clerical elites in Qom saw the anointment of a clerical journeyman as an affront.[13]

Khamenei often is portrayed as being above the fray of factional competition in Iranian politics, although his overt support of Ahmadinejad seems to belie this characterization. He is referred to as an ultimate arbiter: one who allows debate among factions on issues of national import, considers their arguments carefully, and decides on the general guidelines of a course of action, leaving the details of implementation to government councils and ministries. It is also common wisdom that the Supreme Leader wields unquestioned authority over most affairs of state and society in Iran. The reality, however, is some-

---

[12] Tschentscher, 1995, Article 5. The essential qualifications of the Supreme Leader are "a. scholarship, as required for performing the functions of religious leader in different fields; b. justice and piety, as required for the leadership of the Islamic Ummah; c. right political and social perspicacity, prudence, courage, administrative facilities, and adequate capability for leadership" (Tschentscher, 1995, Article 109).

[13] See Sadjadpour, 2008, pp. 5–6.

what less stark. Certainly, the more central an issue—such as the nuclear program or internal security—is to the regime's survival, the more insular the decisionmaking around Khamenei and the less room there is for others to influence the debate. The core decisionmaking group in the area of the nuclear program is comprised of both the Supreme Leader and a subset of heads of the system who sit on the SNSC.[14] Substantive and technical discussions below this level take place at the SNSC and the Foreign Ministry and include a broader group of policymakers and experts. In the area of internal security, it is notable that, since a series of bombings in the Khorasan and Sistan va Baluchistan provinces in 1999–2000, Khamenei has, as commander in chief, swiftly deployed security forces upon sensing any hint of subversion or violence in the provinces. Recent reports indicate that Basiji units are being used to patrol urban areas "to try to help police curb security threats."[15] The Basij played a major role in suppressing the protests after the 2009 presidential election.

In some cases, elements of the elite have defied the edicts and expressed preferences of the Supreme Leader. Reportedly, hard-line members of the judiciary initially rejected Khamenei's call in 2002 to review the death sentence of Hashem Aghajari, a reformist critic of the Islamic system of government, and then "assigned their least lenient judges to the review."[16] More recently, Khamenei had difficulty using his authority to execute a privatization plan that he backed and had supported with a July 2006 change in Article 44 of the constitution (which had banned private ownership of state industries).[17] While meeting with

---

[14] Mehran Kamrava cites Hassan Rowhani as someone who suggested that, in addition to the Supreme Leader himself, the president, the chief nuclear negotiator, and Rafsanjani are among the key decisionmakers on the nuclear issue (Hassan Rowhani, "Farasou-ye Chaleshhaye Iran va Ajans dar Parvandeh-ye Hasteh-ee [Beyond Iran's Difficulties with the Agency Concerning the Nuclear Issue]," *Gofteman*, No. 37, Fall 2005, p. 11, quoted in Kamrava, 2007, p. 96).

[15] "Basij to Help Police Enhance Security in Iran," Fars News Agency, Dialog/World News Connection 0262800517, May 23, 2008.

[16] "International: Hard Centres, Iranian Conservatives," *Economist*, Vol. 365, No. 8304, December 21, 2002, p. 72.

[17] "Privatization a Requirement: Rafsanjani," Mehr News Agency Web site, Dialog/World News Connection 0255750745, January 2, 2008.

cabinet members, he publicly called on the government to "act more seriously in the implementation of the Article 44 privatization plan."[18]

[...] eralization that the Supreme Leader remains [...] me important choices that Khamenei appears [...] Ahmadinejad and the principlists. We provide [...] in Chapter Five. Here, we wish only to note [...] ike an unbiased arbiter and more like a power [...] nce to guide the direction of the state *and* to [...] prerogatives vis-à-vis the political factions [...] stem. In light of Khamenei's clear support [...] sident's allies during the 2009 election, the [...] er claim to be above factional politics.

[...] ows a preference for ideological conserva- [...] uthentic revolutionaries and his natural [...] "resistance" against the United States as [...] on are contained. He recognizes that the [...] attlement is not only a necessary conse- [...] ies but also desirable. An Iran engaged [...] unleash forces bound to affect domestic [...] wn position, and Khamenei's key con- [...] n, which includes his own role.

[...] ader is most comfortable with conser- [...] and anti-Western foreign policies, he tra-
d [...] has ensured that multiple factions, interests, and personalities remain co-opted in the system by maintaining what is a relatively dysfunctional political complex characterized by stalemate among elected and unelected institutions, formal and informal paths of influence, and centers of overlapping power. The greater the balance (or division) among various groups—with no dominant faction that might confidently challenge Khamenei's authority—the more necessary the Supreme Leader's role as broker becomes. Therefore, he encourages factional rivalry as long as it does not threaten the system, which the reformist challenge may have been perceived to do in the 2009 elec-

---

[18] "Leader Calls for More Efficient Implementation of Article 44 Privatization Plan," Mehr News Agency Web site, Dialog/World News Connection 0249300581, August 26, 2007.

tion.[19] Yet Khamenei's strong support of Ahmadinejad and hard-line conservatives has certainly damaged the "balance" in Iranian politics and Khamenei's legitimacy as Supreme Leader.

Undoubtedly, the fact that Khamenei's persona does not match the iconic status held by his predecessor, Khomeini, diminishes the power of the position of Supreme Leader. But Khamenei's influence in the Islamic Republic remains unparalleled (if potentially dimished in the aftermath of the recent election). It reaches far into the government bureaucracy and broader society through the Supreme Leader's representatives, his power of appointment, his control of the mosques and Friday-prayer leaders, and his constitutional authorities, especially as commander in chief of the armed forces.

Other Personalities: Prominence Is Tied to Proximity to the Supreme Leader

Generally, power and influence in Iran are associated with gaining personal proximity to and the confidence of the Supreme Leader. Thus, although the other key personalities among the Iranian elite maintain their own networks of support and patronage, their positions of prominence and influence are strengthened through the support of Khamenei. This is not to say that the Supreme Leader can easily and summarily sack a member of the men's club if that person earns his ire; rather, the member and his allies might find it increasingly difficult to pursue political and economic projects of interest and benefit to them. Khatami is an example of someone who attained a position of great prominence (he was president for two terms) but was foiled in his reform efforts because of the resistance posed by the Supreme Leader and antireform power centers. Still, Khamenei has, in the past, ensured that the members of the men's club remain co-opted in the system so that a balance is maintained among influential networks and factions. It remains to be seen whether the 2009 presidential election and its aftermath have irreparably destroyed this balance.

---

[19] Sources close to the Supreme Leader have occasionally criticized Ahmadinejad for "defaming his political rivals" and reminded him that "such a trend is dangerous for the country" (*Jomhouri-e Eslami* quoted in Nazila Fathi, "Critique of Iranian Leader Reveals Political Rift," *The New York Times*, November 23, 2007a).

A number of the key figures in Iran who were active against the Shah and then played a major role in the Islamic Republic remain influential as heads or members of the Guardian Council, the Expediency Council, clerical associations, and other key institutions. Other, younger personalities entered the elite later and are now key members of the club. The influence, power, and position of most key personalities depend on the Supreme Leader's confidence and patronage. It is not our intent here to list all the members of the men's club, but a review of some of the key personalities will give the reader a sense of their backgrounds, personal ties to the Supreme Leader and other key figures, positions, and influence.

Velayati, who organized physicians against the Shah in the 1970s, originally had no independent base of power, yet he is arguably the closest and most influential advisor to the Supreme Leader on foreign-policy matters. He was the country's foreign minister throughout the 1980s and 1990s (until Khatami's election in 1997). He is also a member of the SCFR and the Expediency Council.[20] Velayati's influence has grown based on his proximity to the Supreme Leader. Former judiciary chief Ayatollah Mahmoud Hashemi-Shahroudi also has little or no power base and depends on Khamenei for his positions and influence. Hashemi-Shahroudi, born in Najaf, Iraq, was a favored protégé of Khomeini. He was a founder of the Supreme Council for the Islamic Revolution in Iraq and is a member of the Assembly of Experts, the Expediency Council, and the Guardian Council. Khamenei appointed him head of the judiciary in 1999, a post he relinquished in 2009 after two five-year terms. It is reported that he exerts influence over Iran's Iraq policy.[21] Other individuals have long-standing ties to the Supreme Leader but also maintain their own power bases. Ayatollah Abbas Va'ez-Tabasi, appointed in 1979 as Khomeini's special representative to Khorasan province and a long-time friend of Khamenei, is the head of one of the richest and most powerful of Iran's *bonyads* (organizations

---

[20] Unpublished research conducted in 2005 by Ray Takeyh and former RAND researcher Daniel Byman.

[21] Posch, 2005b, p. 9. See also Bureau of International Affairs, "Acquaintance with the Head of the Judiciary and His Viewpoints," Web page, undated.

discussed in more detail in a later section). He also serves as a member of the Expediency Council and the Assembly of Experts. His power has earned him the moniker of "Governor of Khorasan," and it is said that he could act self-assuredly and independently of the directives of the central government in Tehran.[22]

Two potential exceptions to the general rule of the confidence of the Supreme Leader being required to maintain great influence in Iran are Ayatollahs Rafsanjani and Ahmad Jannati. Both men command their own powerful networks somewhat independently of Khamenei and, like Khamenei, were protégés of Khomeini and active against the Shah. Rafsanjani's circumstances are very different from those of his peers. Having helped establish the Islamic Republic in 1979 and then served as the first Majles speaker (1980–1989) and president (1989–1997), he is widely perceived to have been Khamenei's kingmaker when the latter was anointed Supreme Leader in 1989. Over the years, Rafsanjani has become a potential rival of Khamenei because of the political clout and enormous wealth he, Rafsanjani, has amassed. (He has close ties with the *bazaari* merchant class, and he and his family are thought to control billions of dollars in assets.) In the two men's public appearances together, Rafsanjani's body language has lacked the deference toward the Supreme Leader exhibited by others.[23] Rafsanjani has been the chairman of the Expediency Council since 1997 and was a presidential candidate in 2005; as the head of the Assembly of Experts since 2007, he now holds a position that, according to the constitution, makes him an overseer of the Supreme Leader's performance. (Whether and how he uses this power remains an open question.) His position also means that he will help select Khamenei's replacement when the current Supreme Leader passes from the scene. However, Rafsanjani's influence may have been diminished by Ahmadinejad's personal attack on him during the 2009 election campaign and by Khamenei's refusal to reply publicly to Rafsanjani's letter, sent three days before the elec-

---

[22] Author telephone discussions with multiple Iran scholars, February and March 2008; unpublished research conducted in 2005 by Takeyh and Byman.

[23] Author telephone discussion with an Iran scholar, March 13, 2008.

tion, requesting that the Supreme Leader "restrain" Ahmadinejad.[24] Rafsanjani's position has been further weakened since the election.

Jannati was active within Khomeini's network in the 1970s and was jailed by the Shah several times. He has been the head of the Guardian Council since 1996 and a member of the Expediency Council and Assembly of Experts. He is also the head of the Haqqani religious school and complex, a well-organized network whose members tend to dominate the judiciary and the MOIS and whose ideological head is Ayatollah Muhammad-Taqi Mesbah-Yazdi. Jannati has built his own considerable financial network and has close relations with the IRGC. He is one of the most politically and socially conservative personalities in Iranian politics, having advocated suicide bombing as a means of resistance, called for Iran to scrap its nuclear-treaty commitments, and championed efforts to export the revolution. He is believed to fund vigilante groups that violently counter reformist and student demonstrations. Jannati maintains influence through his financial assets, his leadership of the powerful Haqqani network, his ties to the IRGC, and his formal position as head of the Guardian Council.[25]

A New Generation

As discussed in an earlier section, a new generation of up-and-coming leaders is now challenging the dominance of the old guard. These new leaders are individuals whom the elder gatekeepers will consider for admittance to the men's club based on the candidates' personal ties and shared worldview. If the old guard comes to see this new generation as members of the club, and if no unforeseen fundamental change in the political system occurs, one can expect these new members to remain on the political scene for the rest of their lives—although not necessarily in the political "clothing" they currently wear. Like their elders, they may remake themselves when necessary to maintain influence among the elite. This new generation is associated with the rise of the IRGC as a political and economic power center, and Ahmadinejad, having

---

[24] See Golnaz Esfandiari, "Rafsanjani Turns to Iran's Supreme Leader to Deal With Ahmadinejad's 'Lies,'" Radio Free Europe/Radio Liberty, June 10, 2009.

[25] Unpublished research conducted in 2005 by Takeyh and Byman.

joined the IRGC in 1986 during the height of the Iran-Iraq War, is the new generation's most visible representative. Other representatives include Larijani, a former member of the IRGC, the current speaker of the Majles, and a close associate of Khamenei; Mohsen Rezai, the commander in chief of the IRGC from 1981–1997, the current secretary of the Expediency Council, and a confidante of Rafsanjani; and Mohammad Baqer Qalibaf, a former IRGC commander, a former chief of the LEF, and the current mayor of Tehran. All three were presidential candidates opposing Ahmadinejad in 2005.[26]

Despite common ties to the IRGC and the Iran-Iraq War, this group of new leaders is by no means monolithic, and its members may part ways on numerous issues. For example, Ahmadinejad's personal rivalries with Larijani and Rezai are well known and often described in Iranian media.

Informal Networks and Patronage Systems of the *Khodi*

Emanating from the Supreme Leader and the other key personalities are concentric circles of influence and power that constitute the *khodi* [one of us]—the insiders—of Iranian society. These are families and dependents, clergy, government and military officials, members of the security apparatus, and well-connected merchants who have some, even tenuous, association with the men's club and derive political, economic, and social benefits from that association. It is estimated that the *khodi* comprise some 15 percent of Iran's population of 66 million citizens.[27] The remainder, the *gheyr-e khodi* [outsiders], includes average citizens and student, women's, and democracy groups aiming to reform or change the Iranian system. Iranian society is, in essence, a two-caste system in which the empowered reap most of the benefits of the system while alternating between cajoling, enlisting, and repressing the powerless. In this sense, Ahmadinejad's style of populist politics is

---

[26] See Wehrey, Green, et al., 2009.

[27] Borzou Daragahi, "Iran's Inner and Outer Circles of Influence and Power," *The Los Angeles Times*, December 31, 2007; Central Intelligence Agency, *The World Factbook: Iran*, 2008.

noteworthy in Iran in that Ahmandinejad portrays himself as *gheyr-e khodi* and spends a great deal of time reaching out to the average citizen for support.[28] Still, Ahmadinejad's influence, position, and, especially, his proximity to and possession of the confidence of Khamenei bestow upon him *khodi* status, as did his involvement in the Revolutionary Guards during the 1980s. *Gheyr-e khodi* can become *khodi* through military service (especially with the Guards) or through the patronage of allies who are already *khodi* and relatively influential.

This small group of elites is far from monolithic; its members derive influence from affiliation with informal networks of individuals and groups with common interests and experiences. These affiliations can be based on familial ties, clerical or educational background, service in the security forces and the Iran-Iraq War, ethnic or regional origin, economic or business interests, and other commonalities. Affiliations are at times issue dependent and temporary. Individuals and groups, including the key personalities described in earlier sections, often associate with and serve as nodes for multiple networks. Thus, a person can derive patronage and influence simultaneously from family ties, service in the Guards, and business connections.[29] Notably, super-networks that combine many types of informal networks may revolve around a common worldview and vision for Iran in the form of political factions, a topic we discuss later in this chapter. Here, it suffices to note that while these political factions compete or cooperate over policy issues, they also serve as vehicles for the aggrandizement of individuals and their allies and networks in their quest for power and influence. As we discuss in Chapter Five, it is through the lens of domestic benefit that many ostensibly political debates can be viewed.

---

[28] During his presidential campaign in 2005, Ahmadinejad portrayed himself as a man of the people and an opponent of the corruption and affluence of the elite. As president, he has made an unprecedented number of extensive visits to all of Iran's provinces. During these visits, state television programs have shown him speaking to and mingling with large crowds and promising to respond to requests for help from average citizens.

[29] For example, Larijani, an advisor to Khamenei and the speaker of the Majles, hails from the family of a prominent cleric; one of Larijani's brothers serves as the head of the judiciary, and another is a member of the Guardian Council. Larijani also has ties to the IRGC and is a former member.

Some key informal networks and power centers in Iran have experienced a cyclical ebb and flow in their level of influence since the revolution. As we describe in the sections that follow, certain networks have eclipsed others at various times, and their dominance tends to endure for about a decade. During periods when one group is dominant, other groups have remained influential, just not to the extent of the dominant group. Still, no one group attains ultimate power in the Iranian system, and the same men's club maintains power. At the outset of the revolution and through the Iran-Iraq War in the 1980s, clerics and their networks had primacy in the Iranian polity. By the 1990s, *bonyads* had become dominant in the economic sphere, though clerics and other types of networks continued to wield a great deal of influence. By the beginning of the current decade, the IRGC and associated groups had begun to arise and to supplant the *bonyads* and clerics as the most influential type of network in Iran.

The 1980s: Era of the Clerics

From the outset of the Islamic Republic, Khomeini established a theocracy in which clerics were dominant in all spheres of government and society. He formed the position of Supreme Leader for one person—himself—to be supported by the Office of the Supreme Leader and the clerical class. Khomeini appointed clerics to senior positions and as special representatives throughout the formal institutional structure. These representatives provided Khomeini with strategic control of key institutions of the state, from the Office of the Supreme Leader at the top to the depths of the bureaucracy at the bottom. Khomeini also centralized control of the mosques and *bonyads* under clerical leadership. As a result, Khomeini was able to enforce his own imprimatur on the overall strategic posture of the state in both the domestic- and foreign-policy spheres.

During the first decade after the revolution, Khomeini's iconic status formed the basis for clerical power. The revolutionary clerics who helped Khomeini realize his vision of an Islamic Republic soon formed powerful groups that projected clerical influence into key parts of government and society. For example, influential conservative clerics organized themselves semiformally in the early 1980s into a Society of Militant Clergy [*jameeh rowhaniyyat-e mobarez*]. Leaders and members of this group soon became dominant in the Guardian Council, the Special Court for the Clergy, and the Assembly of Experts, thereby ensuring conservative control over some of the most-important institutions in the Islamic Republic.[30] They also formed one of the main factional groupings in Iran, the traditional conservatives. (Factions are explored in detail later in this chapter.) In addition, many Friday-prayer leaders, who often serve as the Supreme Leader's representatives to the provinces, currently identify themselves with this camp.

In the 1980s, clerical networks were dominant in many parts of government and society. For example, to start a business, Iranian entrepreneurs had to seek out a powerful patron who could navigate the bureaucracy for the necessary licensure and enable smooth operations; often, this patron would be a cleric. The businessman gained a protector, and the cleric, by offering such services to multiple merchants and others, built a web of patronage upon which he could depend for funds and connections to further business interests.[31]

Clerical establishments remain an important class of networks in Iran today. Notable among these establishments is the aforementioned Haqqani complex of Jannati and Mesbah-Yazdi, which includes theological institutes and cultural foundations in Qom. The Haqqani complex is also a key supporter of Ahmadinejad and his allies. Students of these institutions are groomed for key positions in the judiciary, the MOIS, the Special Court for the Clergy, and the IRGC. Khatami's purge of the MOIS in the late 1990s involved alumni of Haqqani who were implicated in a series of politically motivated murders.[32] These individuals allegedly went on to create parallel security and intelligence institutions in Iran, leading one member of the Majles to claim that "the intelligence apparatus of one of these organs in Tehran has three times the number of personnel that the MOIS has throughout

---

[30] Kamrava, 2007, p. 88.

[31] Author telephone discussions with multiple Iran scholars, February and March 2008.

[32] See Posch, 2005b, pp. 5, 11.

the country."[33] Among Ahmadinejad's earliest ministerial nominees during his first term were Gholamhoseyn Mohseni-Ejei as minister of intelligence and Hojjatoleslam Mustafa Purmohammadi as minister of interior. Both men were alumni of the Haqqani Seminary School in Qom, and Mohseni-Ejei was, until July 2009, the head of the MOIS. The Haqqani network's power over the vetting of political candidates and the tools of repression have led one Western observer to dub the network "the main impediment . . . [to] democracy in Iran."[34]

The 1990s: Era of the *Bonyads*

Having fought a devastating eight-year war with neighboring Iraq and then lost its founding father, the Islamic Republic emerged from the 1980s with serious economic problems and some uncertainty about the future. Khamenei entered his new role as Supreme Leader in 1989 promising to pursue the path that Khomeini had set forth, and Rafsanjani was elected president and empowered with greater authority than his predecessors. With the support of the new Supreme Leader, whom he had helped install, Rafsanjani began a broad reconstruction program, key elements of which involved forging an alliance with the *bazaari* merchants and opening Iran to foreign trade. The alliance was one in which

> the mercantile elites effectively funded the state, mostly through informal and often dubious business arrangements with individual members of the elite and clerical institutions, and in return the state, in the image of President Rafsanjani, supplied an economic environment in which they could make money.[35]

The economic environment shunned government accountability and regulation, and although numerous organizations and interests in Iran could pursue lucrative short-term business ventures unfettered, the

---

[33] Tehran Majles member Mohsen Mirdamadi, *Yas-I No*, July 19, 2003, quoted in Abbas William Samii, "The Iranian Nuclear Issue and Informal Networks," *Naval War College Review*, Vol. 59, No. 1, Winter 2006b, p. 70.

[34] Posch, 2005b, p. 2.

[35] Ali M. Ansari, *Iran Under Ahmadinejad: The Politics of Confrontation*, International Institute for Strategic Studies, *Adelphi Paper* No. 393, 2007, p. 13.

environment was anathema to long-term investments that would have broadened and deepened economic progress in oil-rich Iran. What resulted was, in the words of noted scholar Ali Ansari, "the establishment of informal networks and cartels of business associates, unregulated and avaricious to the extreme."[36]

It was in this environment that the economic influence of the *bonyads* became dominant. *Bonyads* had existed as traditional structures under the Shah, providing humanitarian aid to the poor and other populations in need, but they also served as slush funds for the elite and helped deliver patronage. They continued in a similar role under the Islamic Republic but also greatly expanded their financial resources when they took control of assets confiscated after the revolution from wealthy Iranians and the Pahlavi Foundation.[37] Under Rafsanjani, the *bonyads* controlled and disbursed billions of dollars and greatly enriched those associated with them, using their own wealth to gain patronage, invest in a wide array of business interests, and generally advance their own power and influence. They "monetized" political life in a way the clerics had not during the latter's era of dominance in the 1980s; in a sense, the *bonyads* replaced the clerics as generators of wealth just as a fast-food chain might replace small hamburger franchises (although the clerical establishment retained political dominance).

Moreover, the *bonyads* were (and remain) unaccountable to anyone but the Supreme Leader. For example, Mohsen Rafiqdoost, Khomeini's driver and a relative (by marriage) of Rafsanjani, became a multimillionaire as head of the Foundation of the Oppressed and Disabled [*bonyad-i mostazafan va janbazan*], one of the largest and most well-endowed *bonyads* in Iran. Under Rafsanjani, the foundation became a huge conglomerate of multiple businesses and industries, including tourism, real estate, agriculture, petrochemicals, and transportation. Another powerful *bonyad* is associated with an important religious shrine and pilgrim destination in the northeastern city of Mashhad. Headed by Va'ez-Tabasi, the Imam Reza Shrine Foundation [*astan-i qods-i razavi*] amassed a fortune worth an estimated $15 billion through ventures in

---

[36] Ansari, 2007, p. 14.

[37] Samii, 2006b, p. 67.

automobile manufacturing, agriculture, and real estate and is believed to own 90 percent of the fertile land in Khorasan province.[38]

The *bonyads* became synonymous with the elite avarice against which Ahmadinejad would base his populist message in 2005. Yet they remain very prominent and influential as vehicles for patronage and the enrichment of the elite. At the time of writing in summer 2009, they reportedly controlled an estimated 10–20 percent of Iran's gross domestic product.[39]

The 2000s: Era of the Revolutionary Guards

In the present era, the Revolutionary Guards have become the dominant group not only in traditional defense policy but also in domestic political and economic affairs. The rise of the IRGC has been accompanied by the emergence of core security issues at the forefront of Iranian policy debates (especially the nuclear program, expounded upon in Chapter Five). The IRGC's political emergence began with the organization's episodic confrontations with reform activists during the Khatami administration. The IRGC's political involvement grew as networks of active and retired IRGC officers began to take on an increasingly political role that enabled the IRGC to emerge as a sort of praetorian guard for conservatives seeking to displace Khatami supporters from political power. In the 2003 municipal elections, former IRGC members or associates won a majority of seats on numerous city and town councils, paving the way for their entry into legislative politics during the 2004 parliamentary elections. Many of the 152 new members elected to the Majles in February 2004 had IRGC backgrounds, and 34 former IRGC officers held senior-level posts in the government.[40] During the June 2005 presidential elections, there were,

---

[38] Author telephone discussions with multiple Iran scholars, February and March 2008. See also Katajun Amirpur, "The Future of Iran's Reform Movement," in Walter Posch, ed., *Iranian Challenges*, European Union Institute for Security Studies, Chaillot Paper No. 89, May 2006, p. 32; Wehrey, Green, et al., 2009, pp. 57–59.

[39] Samii, 2006b, p. 67.

[40] Wehrey, Green, et al., 2009. It is unclear whether the IRGC's emergence in Iranian politics is based on some master plan to increase the IRGC's influence or rather on demographic factors as Iran-Iraq War veterans and IRGC personnel come of age (much as U.S. Second

besides Ahmadinejad, three candidates with an IRGC pedigree. At the time of writing, numerous current and former officers with a Guard or Basij background, experience fighting in the Iran-Iraq War, or both were members of the political leadership, including Ahmadinejad, Larijani, Rezai, Ezzatolah Zarghami (head of the Islamic Republic of Iran Broadcasting Corporation), and other cabinet ministers; Majles deputies; provincial governors and mayors; and heads of *bonyads*.[41]

The IRGC has in recent years acquired all the trappings of a state within a state accountable only to the Supreme Leader and increasingly present or even dominant in many facets of society. As the IRGC emerged from fighting Iran's war with Iraq, it became engaged in reconstruction in the 1990s, acquiring a taste for commercial dealings and associated profits. With the election of Ahmadinejad, its position has become more privileged. The IRGC oversees or owns important interests in numerous sectors of the Iranian economy, including oil, construction, agriculture, mining, transportation, defense industry, and import/export. The IRGC's Khatam ol-Anbiya engineering arm is one of Iran's largest industrial contractors, implementing billions of dollars in contracts that include development of the 15th and 16th expansion phases of the South Pars oil field and the extension of the Tabriz Metro.[42] The Guards are also thought to control much of Iran's burgeoning business investment in Dubai, where some 9,000 Iranian businesses are registered and 400,000 Iranian nationals—constituting a quarter of Dubai's population—reside. Iran uses its business investment in Dubai as a means of bypassing international sanctions, and Dubai is commonly referred to as "the best city in Iran."[43] The influence of the IRGC

World War veterans did during the congressional elections of the 1950s and 1960s). It is also important to note that many reformers were former Revolutionary Guards. The Guards were a pool of highly ideological individuals in the 1980s. It is not surprising that, as the Iranian population became disillusioned later on, some of these individuals became reformist leaders.

[41] Mehdi Khalaji, "Iran's Revolutionary Guard Corps, Inc.," *PolicyWatch*, No. 1273, August 17, 2007. See also Wehrey, Green, et al., 2009.

[42] See Wehrey, Green, et al., 2009, pp. 60–61.

[43] Author telephone discussion with an Iran scholar, March 13, 2008.

is now the most sought-after form of patronage in the Islamic Republic for those seeking political or economic benefit, having in some ways eclipsed or displaced the patronage of the clerics.[44]

The Guards have not shied away from blatantly protecting their economic gains. IRGC economic interests played a role in the IRGC's abrupt closure of the new Imam Khomeini International Airport on its first day of operations (May 9, 2004). The IRGC claimed that a Turkish-led consortium, which had been selected to operate the airport, presented a security risk to the state by placing foreign workers at a sensitive transportation node. This episode caused significant international embarrassment to Iran, damaged bilateral relations with Turkey, and hastened the growing impotence of the Khatami administration by forcing the impeachment of Khatami's transportation minister. One of the IRGC's motives for closing the airport was that its own engineering firm had failed to win the contract.[45] In addition, the IRGC may have sought total oversight over the airport's operations as a key transportation hub in the IRGC's illicit smuggling activities.[46]

Thus, the IRGC has, over time, deepened its vested interests in the civilian economy. At the same time, it has retained its primary role as defender of the revolution, a role that continues to be defined expansively as active, often clandestine, involvement in states in the region in support of militias and terrorist groups and, increasingly, participation in domestic politics. The Guards' level of influence in national decisionmaking is difficult to assess, but their intelligence activities would seem to give them an edge over civilian institutions and clerical

---

[44] Author telephone discussion with an Iran scholar, February 26, 2008.

[45] M. P. Zamani, "Perspective: Airport Controversy Goes Sky-High," *Iran Daily* Web site, May 10, 2004, in "Iranian Paper Says Airport Controversy Takes Iran's Internal Divisions 'Sky-High,'" Dialog/World News Connection 0189100393, May 10, 2004; "Shortest Airport Opening in World History," *Iran News* Web site, May 10, 2004, in "Iranian Paper Says Iran's Prestige Damaged by 'Embarrassing' Airport Closure," Dialog/World News Connection 0189100400, May 10, 2004; "Iranian Transportation Ministry Denies Blaming IRGC for Closure of New Airport," Islamic Republic News Agency Web site, Dialog/World News Connection 0194750650, August 31, 2004.

[46] Kim Murphy, "Iran's Guard Builds a Fiscal Empire," *The Los Angeles Times*, August 26, 2007.

interests on specific issues. It would appear that the IRGC's autonomy in some areas, such as Lebanon and Iraq, is both unchallenged and an integral part of Iran's policies. The Guards' authority regarding the nuclear issue is also difficult to evaluate. Although the program was most probably civilian inspired, key nuclear facilities are now managed by the IRGC.[47] U.S. intelligence is reported to have intercepted the Iranian military's objections to Iran's 2003 "halt" in its weaponization program.[48] Growth in the Guards' political influence is likely to keep pace with their rising involvement in national-security decisionmaking and the economy.

The degree to which Khamenei controls the IRGC's foreign and domestic activities also remains unclear. One can rightly point to the fact the Khamenei is commander in chief and has the power to appoint and fire the IRGC's leadership, both of which suggest top-down control of IRGC activities. The reality is probably less black and white. Karim Sadjadpour suggests that the relationship between Khamenei and the IRGC is "increasingly symbiotic, politically expedient for the Leader and economically expedient for the Guards."[49] It is most likely that Khamenei provides overall guidance to the IRGC and that IRGC commanders interpret that guidance in implementing operations and day-to-day activities. As he does with the activities of other institutions in Iran, Khamenei maintains oversight of these IRGC activities through his special representatives and other informal networks. His oversight apparatus enables him to order course corrections if they are needed. The Guards are publicly deferential to the Supreme Leader, and it is unlikely that the IRGC would undertake activities expressly against Khamenei's wishes.

The Revolutionary Guards' increasing political assertiveness in the latter half of the present decade has lead to reformist and even conservative fears of an ongoing militarization of Iranian politics.

---

[47] See Shahram Chubin, *Iran's Nuclear Ambitions*, Washington, D.C.: Carnegie Endowment for International Peace, 2006.

[48] David Sanger and Steve Myers "Notes from Secret Iran Talks Led to Reversal," *International Herald Tribune*, December 7, 2007, p. 4.

[49] Sadjadpour, 2008, p. 8.

Mohammad Ali Jafari, current chief of the IRGC, stated in September 2007 that the "main responsibility" of the Guards had become countering "internal threats," including deviation from the ideology of the Islamic Republic.[50] In February 2008, Jafari stated that the Basij have a "divine responsibility" to support hard-line conservatives (i.e., pro-Ahmadinejad principlists), and his chief of staff added that Iranians should avoid voting for Majles candidates lacking a "revolutionary background."[51] Hossein Ta'eb, deputy commander of the Basij, went so far as to say that his forces would "maximize" voter participation and encourage voters to make "better choices" at the polls.[52] Responses came swiftly from both reformist and conservative quarters. Reformists called Ta'eb's statement an "official declaration of interference," and even Hossein Shariatmadari, managing editor of the progovernment newspaper *Kayhan* (a position gained through the Supreme Leader's appointment), called reformist criticism "unfortunately right" and Jafari's statements a "blatant violation" of the constitution.[53] Even Khomeini's grandson, Seyyed Hasan Khomeini, stated that IRGC involvement in politics would be a "diversion" from his grandfather's legacy.[54] Yet, as the 2009 election dispute has demonstrated, the Revolutionary Guards have become a dominant influence on Iranian politics.

Although the IRGC's most vocal top brass appear to be vociferous supporters of the revolutionary ideal, the Guards are in fact far from monolithic and may be more reflective of Iranian society at large. Factionalism within the IRGC is a continuing part of the landscape. A spectrum of political tendencies is present within both the IRGC leadership and the rank and file, though well defined factions within

---

[50] Reported in Golnaz Esfandiari, "Iran: Warnings Hint at Greater Role by Revolutionary Guard in Muzzling Critics," Radio Free Europe/Radio Liberty, October 5, 2007.

[51] Mohammad Ali Ja'fari, quoted in *E'temad-e Melli* (Tehran), February 9, 2008, in "OSC Analysis: Iran—IRGC Role in Elections Disputed, Khomeyni Legacy Debated," Dialog/World News Connection 0257851460, February 13, 2008.

[52] Ja'fari, 2008.

[53] Ja'fari, 2008.

[54] Ja'fari, 2008.

the Guards are not as apparent. Generally, the older generation appears to be more security-conscious, and it closely adheres to revolutionary ideology. This group views Iran's geostrategic battle against the United States for power and influence across the Middle East as an existential competition that should be the Guards' sole focus. A second group composed of relatively younger IRGC members also perceives a geostrategic competition between Iran and the United States but believes it should be managed at a less-confrontational level in the interest of expanding business opportunities. This business-oriented group is believed to control a significant portion of Iranian business activities in Dubai. Like most large entities, therefore, the IRGC is not monolithic, and its ranks could fracture based on personal interest and worldview.[55]

The IRGC's business activities may pose an additional risk to its internal cohesion. The Guards' rise as an economic power within Iran could taint the organization as a greedy and corrupt force interested in enriching its leaders rather than advancing public welfare and revolutionary ideology. The "5-million-man" Basij could become a source of disaffection in light of the extravagant wealth accumulated by active and former IRGC officers. Although rank-and-file Basijis do receive some benefits for their services, the ability to move to the front of a movie line or attain a slot at a university pales in comparison to the wealth of senior IRGC officers. This disparity may fuel resentment among the lower-class Basijis and may lead to a weakening of their revolutionary resolve and motivation. To prevent dissatisfaction and placate the revolutionary purists among the IRGC and the Basiji rank and file, Iran's leaders may intermittently stir up crises to maintain compliance from the "foot soldiers of the Revolution."[56] Indeed, the recent deployment of Basiji patrols to urban areas reinforces the sense of an ever-present internal-security crisis and serves to ensure that the rank and file are focused on defending the revolution rather than on economic disparities.[57]

---

[55] Author telephone discussion with an Iran scholar, March 13, 2008. See Wehrey, Green, et al., 2009, pp. 81–89.

[56] Author telephone discussion with an Iran scholar, March 13, 2008.

[57] "Basij to Help Police Enhance Security in Iran," 2008.

How the present trend in IRGC influence will play out is difficult to tell. In Chapter Six, we discuss some possible future trajectories and some potentially dominant networks that may supersede the IRGC in the next decade. At this point, our discussion turns to the use of formal institutions as a platform for competition over influence and the state's resources.

Formal Institutional Structure as a Playing Field for Informal Networks

We have characterized some of the peculiarities of Iran's political system, including the parallel existence of elected and unelected institutions and the existence of multiple centers of power that complicate the formulation and implementation of policy. The informal process of politics in Iran can be more influential than its more visible, formal counterpart. As Larijani stated, "the theory of the system" is that it is the person (and his ties), not the post, that is "the origin of power."[58] Although the formal, constitutionally based institutional structure of the Islamic Republic detailed in Chapter Three does provide a framework for governance in Iran, in a more profound sense, it serves as a sort of playing field for the attainment of personal wealth, influence, and prestige. Inversely, through their leadership of, participation in, or association with government ministries or assemblies, powerful individuals also infuse these institutions with a level of influence commensurate with their own influence (and that of their supporting networks).

For example, Rafsanjani has taken advantage of his leadership of the Expediency Council in his rivalry with Ahmadinejad and Ahmadinejad's supporters. In March 2007, Rafsanjani told Iranian journalists that Ahmadinejad's "trial period is over" and that he, Rafsanjani, would use the Expediency Council's supervisory powers to reshape the Ahmadinejad administration's economic policies.[59] Rafsanjani's elec-

---

[58] Ali Larijani, quoted in *Hamshahri Newspaper* (Tehran) in BBC Monitoring, November 11, 2007d.

[59] Robert Tait, "Ahmadinejad Challenged for Control of Iran's Economy," *The Guardian* (London), March 7, 2007.

tion as head of the Assembly of Experts later that year suggested that the assembly could become a more active national player in the future.[60] Just before his election, Rafsanjani reportedly said that "if the Assembly of Experts wants to play a more active role in the country's affairs, it has the religious and legal justification to do that. . . . Perhaps the assembly will do so in its upcoming term."[61] Given his clout in Iranian politics, Rafsanjani's election could foretell a more activist role for the assembly in evaluating the performance of the Supreme Leader and in selecting Khamenei's successor, though he seems to have suffered politically in the aftermath of the 2009 presidential election.

Likewise, as the speaker of the Majles, Larijani has an opportunity to enhance his own prestige by increasing the involvement of the Majles in challenging the policies of Ahmadinejad. Larijani and Ahmadinejad are widely believed to be personal rivals.[62] After the release of an International Atomic Energy Agency (IAEA) report on Iran on May 26, 2008, the Ahmadinejad administration and its supporters portrayed the report as reflecting well on Iran, saying that it did "not contain any negative points."[63] Larijani (and other critics of Ahmadinejad), however, called the IAEA report "deplorable," and Larijani, formerly Iran's chief nuclear negotiator, went on to warn that the Majles would "definitely get involved" in future matters pertaining to Iran's dealings with the IAEA.[64] Larijani appeared to be taking on Ahmadinejad over an issue that the president has very clearly exploited in his rhetoric to gain support and whip up nationalism. The status of the Majles could therefore be enhanced due to the personal influence and experience of

---

[60] See Vahid Sepehri, "Iran: Political Veteran to Chair Clerical Assembly," Radio Free Europe/Radio Liberty, September 7, 2007.

[61] Rafsanjani, quoted in Islamic Republic News Agency, reported in Ali Akbar Dareini, "Rafsanjani to Head Iranian Clerical Body," Associated Press, September 4, 2007.

[62] See Nazila Fathi and Graham Bowley, "New Post for Rival of President of Iran," *The New York Times*, May 29, 2008.

[63] Mohammad Ali Hoseyni, quoted in Fars News Agency, June 1, 2008, in "OSC Report: Iran—Critics Use IAEA Report to Suggest Larger Role for Majles," Dialog/World News Connection 263451475, June 5, 2008.

[64] Hoseyni, 2008.

its speaker, although its status would likely change when Larijani leaves his post and a new speaker is selected.

Foreign Minister Manouchehr Mottaki is an example of an individual who gained and retained his position because of his ties to Khamenei's inner circle. A ministry insider described by one scholar as "a second-tier apparatchik,"[65] Mottaki did not support the 2005 presidential candidacy of Ahmadinejad, who reportedly sought to oust Mottaki despite having nominated him to the position of foreign minister after becoming president.[66] These efforts were to no avail because of Mottaki's relationship with Velayati, foreign minister to Presidents Mir Hossein Mousavi and Rafsanjani in the 1980s and 1990s, who exerts considerable influence in the ministry and is a primary foreign-policy advisor to the Supreme Leader.[67] Thus, the foreign minister, a person who constitutionally serves at the pleasure of the president (with oversight from the Majles), remains at his post, apparently despite the president's objections. And, Mottaki is overshadowed by a former foreign minister who has no formal power.

In sum, the formal institutions of the state serve primarily as vehicles of influence for personalities and power centers while at the same time providing the formal structure for implementation of state policy. The overlapping nature of the institutions' authorities seems to be a natural extension of the informal processes behind them: Just as the system is designed so that no informal power center gains excessive power within the state, so too are formal institutions constrained. As the broker who manages and oversees this system, the Supreme Leader thus maintains his authority. This balancing also applies to the factional clusters that are such an important part of the political landscape in Iran, a topic to which we now turn.

---

[65] Author telephone discussion with an Iran scholar, February 26, 2008. Mottaki was the head of the Majles committee on foreign relations and security at the time of his selection, and he had been a deputy foreign minister and ambassador for many years before that. See International Crisis Group "Iran: Ahmadinejad's Tumultuous Presidency," *Middle East Briefing*, No. 21, February 6, 2007, p. 3, fn. 6.

[66] Walter Posch, "Only Personal? The Larijani Crisis Revisited," Centre for Iranian Studies, Durham University, Policy Brief No. 3, November 2007, p. 9.

[67] Posch, 2007, p. 5.

Factions: Supernetworks of Individuals, Relationships, and Power Centers

The cooperation and competition among factions that occurs behind the scenes of the formal political structure tend to drive policymaking in the Islamic Republic. Four main factions—here defined as fluid political groupings of like-minded influential personalities, families, clerical institutions, societies, and political parties that transcend familial, experiential, and other personal associations—appear to dominate the political landscape in Iran. One can view these factions as combinations of key individuals and informal networks under supernetworks that espouse common worldviews, visions for the Islamic Republic, and policy preferences. All four of these factions support *velayat-e faqih*— any group overtly agnostic or antagonistic toward this central tenet of the Islamic Republic would of course be excluded from the ranks of the *khodi* and from political life altogether—and agree on the need for the Islamic Republic to maintain its sovereignty, regional status, economic power, and access to technology.

Nevertheless, these factions vie with one another to gain privilege and influence within the agreed-upon political system. In fact, the nature of the system effectively promotes and entrenches factional rivalry. Moreover, individual groups or subfactions identified as part of a faction do not necessarily follow a party line on all issues, and, thus, the factions' composition may change depending on the issue at stake. As a way of gaining prestige and political or economic influence, groups in one faction may pursue alliances with groups in other factions, or they may compete with groups within their own faction based on specific interests. And, as noted previously, key individuals may remake themselves over time in ways that alter their associations with certain factions.[68] The intense factional rivalry inherent in the Iranian system makes for a lively and at times acrimonious political

---

[68] Rafsanjani, for example, was considered a reactionary under Khatami's presidency; today, however, the Rafsanjani (pragmatic conservative) and Khatami (reformist) factions have found many issues around which to ally. To employ a sports analogy, political factions in Iran are not teams that show up with the same players at every game; rather, teams form based on the game to be played.

environment in which multiple groups vie for expanded control of the state and its resources.

For the purposes of our discussion, we divide Iran's ideological factions into four categories: traditional conservatives, reformists, pragmatic conservatives, and principlists.[69] Although the Office of the Supreme Leader and other key institutions have generally remained the purview of the traditional conservatives, each of the other factions has enjoyed a period of formal political power through its control, at one time or another, of the Majles and the presidency.

Traditional conservatives, who constitute the largest faction, advocate clerical rule, consolidation of the revolution's gains, a traditional Islamic lifestyle, and Iranian economic and technological self-sufficiency. This faction finds support among the lower-middle classes, lower-ranking clerics, and many *bazaari* merchants. Traditional conservatives dominate the Guardian Council, the Assembly of Experts, and the Special Court for the Clergy. Most Friday-prayer leaders and other special representatives of the Supreme Leader are traditional conservatives. The faction's key formal organizations include the Association of Qom Seminary Teachers and the Society of Militant Clergy.[70]

Despite his professed position above the factional fray, Khamenei appears to identify most closely with the traditional conservatives, although he also demonstrates comfort with the principlists. Other key personalities associated with the traditional conservative faction have included Ayatollah Ali Akbar Feyz Meshkini (the head of the Assembly of Experts until his recent death) and Ayatollah Va'ez-Tabasi (the Supreme Leader's representative to Khorasan province and the head of the Imam Reza Shrine *bonyad*).

The **reformist movement** emerged in the mid-to-late 1980s around a group of clerics with more-moderate views of Iranian social, economic, and foreign policies than those held by conservatives who,

---

[69] This typology draws from RAND discussions with a number of scholars of Iran, a RAND-sponsored workshop in Rome, Italy, and internal RAND research. See Green, Wehrey, and Wolf, 2009. See also Kamrava, 2007, pp. 84–100; Walter Posch, "Islamist Neo-Cons Take Power in Iran," Occasional Paper No. 3, Ljubljana Institute for Security Studies, July 2005a; Buchta, 2000, pp. 11–21.

[70] See Kamrava, 2007, p. 88.

along with the new reformists, had shepherded and solidified the revolution. Reformists argued for the promotion of civil society, a relaxation of political and social controls, economic openness, and more interaction with the outside world under the guise of a so-called dialogue of civilizations. The apex of reformist influence occurred in the mid-1990s when the faction attained a majority in the Majles and then gained the presidency under Khatami. Although the faction has been popular with the intelligentsia and students, its popular support has never translated into successful pursuit of its agenda, which was thwarted at every turn by more–politically conservative elements in the Iranian polity (including the Supreme Leader himself). Notably, the IRGC began its ascendancy as a political and economic power center during Khatami's administration.

Generally, reformists favor a relatively moderate foreign policy and broad-based relations with the West; to them, the success of the revolution is tied to less-confrontational policies at the regional and international levels. They support pursuit of a nuclear program but in the context of improved relations with the international community. They also want Iran to make economic progress through integration into the global economy, a stronger private sector, and attraction of foreign investment.

The reformists have been under constant political pressure and criticism from the traditional conservatives and principlists since they were ousted in the Majles elections of 2004 and Ahmadinejad became ascendant in 2005. The Guardian Council has used its election-oversight powers to veto hundreds of reformist candidates for Majles seats. In the summer of 2008—a full nine months before the March 2009 elections—Ahmadinejad supporters warned Khatami not to run for president.[71] Moreover, newspapers and student groups that identify with the reformist faction have been harassed and, in some cases, shut down by the authorities or by vigilante groups. Reformists are being marginalized in the aftermath of the recent election.

---

[71] "Iran's Khatami Warned About Possible Run for President," Radio Free Europe/Radio Liberty, July 30, 2008. Shariatmadari wrote that if Khatami were to announce his candidacy for president, the Guardian Council would disqualify him.

The **pragmatic conservatives**—among whom Rafsanjani is a central figure—tend to believe in top-down economic modernization and argue for technical and financial cooperation with the West, including the United States. Despite harboring some suspicions about U.S. motives and intentions, the pragmatic conservatives appear to view slowly warming relations with the West as a key to improving Iran's economy and global standing. Therefore, this faction has much in common with the reformists on economic- and foreign-policy issues. However, unlike the reformists, the pragmatic conservatives show little interest in liberalization of the political system. On cultural issues, the pragmatic conservatives span a wide range of tendencies, with some supporting, through the Executives of Construction Party [*hezbe kargozaran sazandegi*] the reformists' approach and others leaning, through the Justice and Development Party [*hezbe e'tedal va tose'eh*] toward the traditional conservatives on cultural issues. The pragmatic conservatives have traditionally derived support from elements of the *bazaari* merchant class, some students, the urban middle classes, and technocrats. In recent years, the pragmatists have made a de facto alliance with the reformists against the pro-Ahmadinejad principlists over a number of key foreign- and economic-policy issues.

The **principlist** faction has been most closely identified with the ascendancy of the IRGC in Iranian politics, beginning with the gains of IRGC alumni and allies in the 2003 local elections and leading up to the election of Ahmadinejad in 2005. The principlist faction is made up of various subsections, including the Developers of Islamic Iran [*abadgaran-e iran-e eslami*], which was comprised of IRGC and Basiji war veterans. Many of these veterans rose to mid- and senior-level positions but were subsequently marginalized during the Rafsanjani era. During the 2005 presidential election, the principlists appealed mostly to the urban poor and provincial classes and depicted themselves as remaining steadfast to the revolution's ideals. At the time of writing, they dominated the executive branch of government under Ahmadinejad and retained a considerable number of seats in the Majles. Figures other than Ahmadinejad who consider themselves principlists include Larijani and Sa'id Jalili, the secretary of the SNSC and the chief nuclear negotiator. Many principlists are highly devout laypeople and, at times, have challenged (through, for example, their use of messianic imagery and their denunciations of corruption and the enrichment of some clerics) the dominance of the clerical elite among the traditional conservatives. Yet on political and social issues, they often agree with the traditional conservatives, and they do draw clerical support from the influential Haqqani complex and conservative clerics, such as Mesbah-Yazdi and Jannati.

The principlists tend to advocate a return to the "pure" principles of the revolutionary era and, like the traditional conservatives, preach Iranian self-reliance and technical independence. Principlists believe in the Islamization of society in all matters, including art and culture, and appear to pursue egalitarian, state-centered economic policies that favor the redistribution of wealth to the poor and the downtrodden. Naturally, they are suspicious of reformists and pragmatic conservatives, who seek political, social, religious, and economic reforms. They also appear to be very suspicious of the West and to value alliances with non-Western nations, such as Russia and China. On the nuclear issue, the principlists emphasize Iran's indisputable right to pursue nuclear enrichment, and they portray international disagreement over the program as a technical issue that should be dealt with by the IAEA, although, recently, even the IAEA's activities in Iran face restrictions.

A number of fissures have appeared in the principlist faction over the perception that Ahmadinejad's government has been "neglecting the people, breaking the law and making use of revolutionary and religious values for the sake of material gain."[72] The March 2008 Majles elections reflected the divisions among the principlists, who formed a political bloc, the United Principlist Front, to defeat the reformists. Meanwhile, Ahmadinejad supporters organized under a subfaction, the Sweet Scent of Service, and attempted to steer the selection process for principlist candidates, producing friction among their principlist cohorts. Some of the intrafactional maneuvering could be interpreted

---

[72] Anonymous member of the "Independent Principle-ists' Current," quoted in *Farhang-e Ashti* (Tehran), February 7, 2008, in "OSC Analysis: Iran—Rifts Among Conservatives Intensify as Elections Approach," Dialog/World News Connection 0258501457, February 26, 2008.

as the machinations of key players positioning themselves to run in the June 2009 presidential election. Principlist critics of Ahmadinejad have included Larijani, former Majles speaker Haddad-Adel, and mayor of Tehran and former IRGC commander Qalibaf. All three have been emphasizing good management of the government and have been burnishing their academic credentials in an attempt to contrast themselves with Ahmadinejad, who is perceived as less educated and more simple-minded.[73]

Traditional conservative clerics have also entered the fray, demonstrating the factional, generational, and religious rivalry between the old men's club and the younger leadership generation, including Ahmadinejad and his supporters. Ayatollah Mohammad Reza Mahdavi-Kani, the 77-year-old head of the Society of Militant Clergy, member of the Assembly of Experts, and traditional conservative icon, has supported principlist figures opposed to the Ahmadinejad administration. Mahdavi-Kani has strongly criticized Ahmadinejad for his handling of the economy and has asked Ahmadinejad "not to presume the clergy . . . [are] tools" or "attempt to undermine the status of the clergy and elders."[74] Elements of both the Society of Militant Clergy and the traditional conservative Qom Seminary Lecturers' Association also backed Larijani for the Majles speakership. Larijani's victory was the first time a candidate from Qom beat a candidate from Tehran for this very important position.

The 2009 election dispute demonstrated both the deep schism within the conservative camp and the traditional clergy's opposition to Khamenei and to Ahmadinejad's policies. Key conservative figures, such as Rafsanjani, emerged as part of the "opposition" to Ahmadinejad's

---

[73] Author telephone discussion with an Iran scholar, March 4, 2008. See also "Iran: Conservatives Claim Victory, but President Faces New Challenges," Radio Free Europe/Radio Liberty, March 17, 2008; Anonymous member of the "Independent Principle-ists' Current," 2008.

[74] Mohammad Reza Mahdavi-Kani, quoted in Shahab News Agency, April 17, 2008, in "OSC Analysis: Iran—Conservative Elders Join in Factional Maneuvering," Dialog/World News Connection 0261401423, April 25, 2008b. Given the rivalry between Larijani and Ahmadinejad, one can speculate that the latter may no longer have the support of some major clerical figures in Qom.

"reelection." Even Larijani, who is considered to be close to Khamenei, issued a statement asking the security forces to be kind to the demonstrators, implying that he was not entirely happy with the government's response to the protests. Moreover, such high-ranking clergymen as Grand Ayatollah Nasir Makarem-Shirazi asked for "national conciliation," demonstrating that many of the high-ranking clergy in Qom did not approve of Ahmadinejad's reelection and the government's handling of the crisis.[75] The anti-Ahmadinejad reaction from within the conservative movement represents general dissatisfaction with the government's overall decisionmaking processes, which have become restricted to a group of key Ahmadinejad supporters with access to Khamenei. Such is the state of politics in Iran that even such figures as Rafsanjani and Larijani perceive themselves as having been marginalized from Khamenei's inner circle.

Concluding Remarks: Factionalism and Informal Networks

In sum, the Iranian political system is a composite of key personalities and associated informal networks and power centers, all of which often unite over common interests in the form of political factions. Members of these networks occupy and exploit positions in formal government institutions. A number of key personalities (including, first and foremost, Khamenei) have dominated the political elite in Iran since the 1979 revolution and Khomeini's death in 1989. These personalities draw on multiple commonalities—familial, experiential, clerical, political, financial, and other relationships and interests—to generate economic and political support and patronage and, at times, dissent. Key individuals, such as Rafsanjani, have used their positions in government to enrich themselves and to become important sources of patronage for their families, allies, and networks. And, the more powerful, influential, and well-connected the individual or individuals leading a

---

[75] "Iran: Senior Cleric Favours 'National Conciliation' After Post-Election Unrest," *Iran Online*, Dialog/World News Connection 0283200022, July 5, 2009.

government institution are, the greater the weight the institution gains in policymaking and implementation within Iran.[76]

The very informality of the system makes the examination of Iranian decisionmaking exceedingly difficult because back-channel maneuvering and bargaining are, by nature, hidden from public view. But the factional maneuvering that defines decisionmaking in the Islamic Republic is indeed manifested publicly at times, especially during crisis. It is therefore possible to discern differences in outlook and to gain insight into what motivates actors or groups in Iran to take their positions on major issues of the day. In the next chapter, we examine factional competition in the context of key foreign- and domestic-policy issues.

---

[76] In some ways, this is not unlike some institutions in the U.S. government. Contrast Colin Powell's challenges as Secretary of State during President George W. Bush's first term—especially in relation to much-more-influential personalities, including Vice President Dick Cheney and Secretary of Defense Donald Rumsfeld—with early indications that Hillary Clinton, a former senator, key presidential candidate, and first lady, will be a powerful Secretary of State under Obama.

CHAPTER FIVE

The Nexus of Domestic Politics and Policymaking in Iran

Having reviewed Iran's strategic culture, the formal constitutional framework of the Iranian regime, and the informal networks that drive leadership dynamics in Tehran, we assess in this chapter how these dynamics work in the context of foreign- and domestic-policy issues critical to the Islamic Republic.

Iran's foreign policy has often been shaped by the political and ideological conflicts between various factions, particularly since the death of Khomeini in 1989. This process has produced both periods of pragmatism and moderation in Iran's approach to the outside world and, conversely, periods of confrontation and defiance. (The presidency of Ahmadinejad has ushered in the latter type of environment.) Two important foreign-policy case studies put flesh on these observations. The Middle East issue is the touchstone of Iran's foreign relations, reflecting the country's insistence on serving as a role model for the Islamic world and, in particular, for Iran's Arab neighbors. The nuclear issue has been called the most difficult—more difficult even than Iran's war with Iraq—ever faced by the Islamic Republic.[1] The stakes associated with the nuclear issue have been inflated to encompass a test of Iran's identity and a referendum on the Islamic Republic itself. The next section provides general insights into the formulation of foreign and security policy in the Islamic Republic and the role of factions in

---

[1] See Chubin, 2006; Shahram Chubin, "Iran: Domestic Politics and Nuclear Choices," in Ashley Tellis and Michael Wills, eds., *Strategic Asia 2007–2008: Domestic Political Change and Grand Strategy*, Washington, D.C.: National Bureau of Asian Research, 2007.

policymaking. Then, we analyze the influence of informal politics on Iran's policies toward the rest of the Middle East and dealings with the international community over the nuclear program. Finally, we explore the role of Iran's economy as a battleground for personal and factional rivalries and offer some concluding remarks.

Foreign Policy as a Backdrop for Domestic Politics

As we indicated in previous chapters, the primary arena for political competition among elites is the domestic sphere, and this competition is as much about power as about principles or policies. Given domestic priorities, foreign policy is used to bolster domestic positions or weaken factional rivals. Rivals can be discredited for endangering the system and for not pursuing revolutionary precepts—i.e., for selling out. By the same token, positions adopted clearly reflect domestic preferences.

Domestic considerations and rivalries have been foremost in the major decisions taken by the Islamic Republic at different times. Islamist revolutionaries used the 1979–1980 hostage crisis to strengthen the radical factions of the revolutionary movement; the 1989 decision to issue a *fatwa* against Salman Rushdie resulted from conservatives' attempts to limit Iran's opening to the world; and the decision to end the war with Iraq was made because prolongation of the war was threatening to become dangerous for the stability of the Iranian regime.[2] Shaping foreign policy to serve domestic and factional objectives is, thus, no novelty in Iranian politics. Under Ahmadinejad, the principlists have used the technique in an attempt to undermine their reformist and pragmatic conservative rivals and paint them as weak, defeatist, and insufficiently revolutionary. At the same time, Ahmadinejad has posed as the leader of Iran's resistance against so-called arrogant outside

---

[2]   At the beginning and through much of the war, the Iranian regime used the conflict to consolidate power, suppress internal opposition, and rally public support. The war was also seen as an opportunity to extend the revolution to Iraq. But, as Iranian losses piled up and the United States entered the conflict (incapacitating the Iranian Navy in Operation Praying Mantis in 1988), Khomeini was persuaded to come to terms in the interest of the regime's stability. See Wehrey, Green, et al., 2009.

powers (especially the United States) that seek to keep Iran down. This policy of provoking deliberate confrontation is rooted in a domestic calculation of benefit. The president has not been disappointed in the effects of his policy and has, in the past, been openly supported by the Supreme Leader, who, in 2008, warmly endorsed pro-Ahmadinejad candidates in the parliamentary elections, and Ahmadinejad himself in the aftermath of the 2009 presidential election.[3]

Since the inception of the Islamic Republic, revolutionary slogans and posturing that characterize Iran as an Islamic model and exemplary state have been an integral part of foreign policy. This revolutionary identity was important to maintain public support for the regime, and it became an integral part of the regime's legitimacy. As successive governments proved unable to substitute this identity with normalcy and legitimacy based on performance (especially in the economic sphere), "permanent revolution," at least in foreign-policy slogans, appeals, and selective actions, became indispensable. The government's incentive to use foreign policy for domestic political considerations has increased as its ability to meet domestic expectations has decreased. Foreign-policy issues, such as the nuclear program, have the convenient feature of diverting attention away from mundane, "bread-and-butter" issues to questions of identity, existence, and principles. For example, in the 2008 Majles elections, the Ahmadinejad government used foreign policy to minimize its domestic failings and focus on its "brave resistance" against perceived external threats, and the president again used this tactic during the campaign for the June 2009 presidential election. Foreign policy is also used to paint domestic critics as foreign agents and justify repression.

There are certain fundamental Iranian foreign-policy propositions that provoke little dissent. For example, Iranians support an independent foreign policy that accords with their perception of the stature of

---

[3] See, inter alia, Ansari, 2007; Michael Slackman "Iranian Uses Crises to Solidify His Power; Feud with West Fuels Ahmadinejad," *International Herald Tribune*, September 5, 2007a; Najmeh Bozorgmehr and Roula Khalaf, "Supreme Leader Keeps Watchful Eye as Ahmadinejad Consolidates Power," *Financial Times* (London), October 25, 2007b; Najmeh Bozorgmehr, "Ayatollah Ensures Results Confirm His Absolute Supremacy," *Financial Times* (London), March 19, 2008b.

the country and enhances Iran's security and development prospects. It has been suggested that the revolution created a new identity in which "anti-imperialism emerged as a central institution of Iran's foreign policy culture" and that "the Iranian republic adheres to certain grand strategic preferences that transcend the fault lines of day-to-day politics."[4] In this view, challenging the status quo and the United States' dominant position is an intrinsic part of Iranian revolutionary "culture," and this "culturally constituted consensus" transcends political factionalism.[5] It is certainly true that revolutionary rhetoric persists and that the anti-imperialist nature of the revolution continues to be an important theme.[6] Other themes, such as solidarity with the dispossessed or the oppressed, especially Muslims, also continue to resonate culturally.

Factional Policy Differences

There may, however, be less agreement about the proper path to take on the core security issues—such as the nuclear issue, the projection of Iranian power in the Persian Gulf, and Iranian intervention in Iraq— than meets the eye. Disagreement among factions springs from more-fundamental concerns than mere discomfort over Ahmadinejad's presentation of issues and style.[7] Indeed, there are different opinions on virtually all security issues, except perhaps the belief that Hezbollah is a legitimate national actor worthy of Iran's support (but the nature of that support is a divisive topic).[8] Foreign and security policy are neither

---

[4]   Arshin Adib-Moghaddam, "Islamic Utopian Romanticism and the Foreign Policy Culture of Iran," *Critique: Critical Middle East Studies*, Vol. 14, No. 3, Fall 2005, p. 284.

[5]   Adib-Moghaddam, 2005, p. 285.

[6]   Olivier Roy emphasizes the anti-imperialist theme in the revolution. See Oliver Roy, *The Politics of Chaos in the Middle East*, New York: Columbia University Press, 2008, p. 130.

[7]   Some observers argue that the disagreement centers on Ahmadinejad's coarse and sometimes undiplomatic expression of Iranian policies. See, for example, David Mack, Patrick Clawson, Hillary Man Leverett, and Ray Takeyh, comments at "Iran on the Horizon, Panel IV: Iran: What Does the U.S. Do Now?" Middle East Institute Conference Series, Middle East Institute, Washington, D.C., February 1, 2008.

[8]   For an excellent analysis, see Kamrava, 2007, p. 92. Kamrava notes that there are disagreements over five of six policy issues (the sixth being Hezbollah: the Middle East, Iraq, the nuclear program, the United States, and Hamas).

a blank slate nor set in concrete; there are choices to be made, and they are made by a divided elite who, as we demonstrate in the following paragraphs, have different conceptions of where Iran ought to go and how it should get there.

Although there may be consensus among factions and interest groups on general principles, such as allegiance to the Islamic Republic and the need for independence or resistance, such consensus belies the fundamental differences within the leadership that agitate below the surface. These differences stem from different views of (1) the world as it is, (2) the relationship between foreign and domestic politics, (3) Iran's priorities and the role Iran should play in the region and the world, and (4) the proper use of diplomacy and slogans. Broadly speaking, there are two opposing views of how Iran should approach the outside world: There are those (mainly the reformists and some pragmatic conservatives) who want to ease Iran into the global system, and there are those (including pro-Ahmadinejad principlists) who wish to pursue revolutionary goals. In general, the first group sees the necessity for Iran to develop into a normal state, a path that requires Iran to be at peace with the international community and to espouse a moderate foreign policy. The second group sees Iran as a revolutionary state that should adopt an assertive foreign policy in defense of Islamic interests, rally domestic and regional forces, and create social justice through the redistribution of the country's oil wealth and the marginalization of those considered insufficiently revolutionary. These very important differences are likely to be in contention in the Islamic Republic for some time and were certainly strongly manifested in the contentious 2009 presidential election.

Rowhani, former national security advisor and chief nuclear negotiator under Khatami, has observed that Iranians "still have not reached an agreement on many problems, on how to conduct our foreign policy, on how to deal with our interlocutors, on how to present our policies to the world opinion" and "are still debating whether we should place development or justice at the center of our focus"—

i.e., whether to behave as a state or as a revolution.[9] Taking the view that Iran's state interests should be paramount, he argues that development, to be sustainable, requires security and self-confidence and, therefore, a moderate foreign policy:[10]

> In our foreign policy, do we want to be ambiguous or clear, do we want the region and the world to be afraid of us or to be our friends, do we want to become every day more fearful or more attractive? . . . If we consider the Islamic Revolution as the top priority, then we should be aware that we will be carrying an extremely grave responsibility on our shoulders. In other words, we are the Islamic Revolution and we want to spread this culture across the region and the Islamic world as a whole. However, if we seek to be primarily the Islamic Republic of Iran, our foremost mission and priority will be the Islamic Republic of Iran, and that means we will traverse a different path.[11]

Ahmadinejad and many principlists agree that there are two approaches to the revolution: One approach sees the revolution as a historical phenomenon, subject to the passage of time and hence a closed chapter. The other approach, as expressed by Ahmadinejad, considers the revolution to be

---

[9] See Hassan Rowhani, "20 Years Perspectives and a Progressive Foreign Policy," *Persian Journal*, February 28, 2008a; "Khamenei's Leadership Challenged by Mr. Hasan Rowhani," Iran Press Service, February 29, 2008. See also Hassan Rowhani, interview with Iranian Student's News Agency, November 22, 2008, in BBC Monitoring, November 27, 2008b. In criticizing Ahmadinejad's "simplistic" populism, Khatami observed that it was not "right to reduce justice to economic justice. The wealth of the country should add to the wealth and power of the country and then redistribute it" (Nazila Fathi "Former Iranian President Publicly Assails Ahmadinejad," *The New York Times*, December 12, 2007b).

[10] For a thoughtful presentation along these lines, see Mohammad Nahavandian, quoted in *E'temad-e Melli* (Tehran) Web site, in "Nahavandian: Moderation in Foreign Policy is the Only Way Towards Development," Dialog/World News Connection 0259100818, March 10, 2008. Nahavandian, the chair of the Iranian Chamber of Commerce, made the presentation to a conference at the Strategic Studies Center of the Expediency Council.

[11] Rowhani, 2008a. See also, "Iran Press: Ex-Nuclear Chief Criticizes 'Ideological' Impact on Foreign Policy," Baztab News & Information Center Web site quoted on *E'temad-e Melli* (Tehran) Web site, July 23, 2006, in BBC Monitoring, July 24, 2006.

a social truth and a necessary belief. Revolution is an upheaval and constant improvement to reach pinnacles of personal and social perfection. . . . The first approach believes that remaining revolutionary is a kind of *extremis*, adventurousness, and even breaking the law, but the second approach believes that Revolution is a type of lasting reform and a foundation which demands continuous efforts [jihad].[12]

Different views on how Iran should deal with the world stem from different views on what Iran should become. It is no surprise, therefore, to see divergence of opinion about how Iran should conduct itself—i.e., with diplomacy and tact or provocation and defiance. Rowhani distinguished between the two schools of thought using the nuclear issue as an example: There were moderates who believed that, although the United States was weakened by Iraq, the nuclear controversy (especially in the UN Security Council) could continue to cause Iran serious problems and, hence, they saw a need to defuse the controversy through discussion and flexibility; then, there were principlists who saw a weakened United States as an opportunity to use Iran's newfound regional influence to avoid discussions and continue to press on its current course without reference to the concerns of others.[13] The first group sought to reassure others about Iran's aims and reduce the possibility of isolation and sanctions; the other welcomed confrontation "wrapped up in a critical assertive foreign policy" which disowned its predecessors' "passive diplomacy."[14]

---

[12] Mahmoud Ahmadinejad, quoted on the Hemayat Web site, March 10, 2008, in "Iran Commentary Speaks on Different Approaches to Revolution," BBC Monitoring, March 11, 2008c.

[13] Hassan Rowhani, interview with *Tehran-e Emrooz* (Tehran), December 13, 2007, in BBC Monitoring, December 15, 2007b.

[14] Contrast Rowhani's comment—"we must not do anything to increase our enemies"—with that of Foreign Ministry spokesman Mohammad Ali Hoseyni, who euphemistically called the Ahmadinejad approach "active diplomacy" necessary "to deal with bullying powers." For Rowhani's quote, see Hassan Rowhani, "Sense of Owning the Country and People, Our Incurable Ailment," *Aftab-e Yazd* (Tehran) Web site, October 11, 2007, in "Iran Cleric Calls for National Unity, Raising 'Tolerance Threshold' to Criticism," BBC Monitoring, October 14, 2007a. For Hoseyni's quote, "Iran's Aggressive Foreign Policy Based on

Whatever one's beliefs, there is little doubt that the tone and content of the Ahmadinejad government's approach to diplomacy has aggravated elite rivalries and caused a deterioration of political discourse that constrains debate "at the national level."[15] The principlists have depicted the reformists and pragmatic conservatives as defeatists and foreign agents, and the latter have accused the government of propelling the country toward war. This has made the outcome of the debate on key foreign policy issues a much more important consideration in the domestic fortunes of the respective groups. Hence, success or failure abroad could buttress or weaken their domestic bases of power.

Iranian Policy in the Middle East: Factional Determinants and Geopolitical Context

In looking at the Islamic Republic's Middle East policy, we analyzed whether and how the policy under Ahmadinejad differs from the policy under past governments. What are the changes, and what were their principal causes? Specifically, to what extent are these changes the result of domestic factors rather than evolution of the regional environment, the balance of power, U.S. policy, or other factors? We also examined the role of factionalism in determining regional policies.

Iran's policy toward the Middle East has taken a distinct and deliberate turn since 2005; increasingly "provocative" regarding the West, Iran has left the "middle ground and sought to lead the rejectionist camp" while making "anti-Israeli rhetoric one of the defining characteristics of . . . [Ahmadinejad's] presidency."[16] The cause of this

---

Wisdom," Islamic Republic News Agency Web site, December 10, 2007, in BBC Monitoring, December 10, 2007.

[15] Mohammad Javad Kashi, "Iran Paper Says Structure of 'Political Discourse' Undergoing Change," *Mardom-Salari* (Iran) Web site, November 28, 2007, in BBC Monitoring, December 1, 2007.

[16] Roy, 2008, pp. 126–127. Roy also observes that "the deliberate choice of provocation" marks "one more milestone in bringing Iran into a phase of conflict with the West." For the personalities and positions of the rejectionist camp leadership, see Anoush Ehteshami and Mahjoob Zweiri, eds., *Iran's Foreign Policy: From Khatami to Ahmadinejad*, Ithaca, N.Y.:

policy shift is the coincidence of a principlist government in Tehran and a change in the regional environment. The current government marks a major discontinuity from that of its predecessors under Rafsanjani and Khatami. The principlist groups that dominate the current regime rely on the IRGC, the Basij, the lower religious classes, and the rural population rather than the urban middle class, students, or technocrats, who tended to support the reformists and pragmatic conservatives under Khatami and Rafsanjani. The Ahmadinejad administration also enjoys the support of the Supreme Leader, who has actively sought to undercut the reformists and may distrust Rafsanjani.

The regional environment has also favored the principlist approach to foreign policy. Here, we wish only to note that Arab frustration and insecurity, combined with the perceived decline of U.S. influence in the region, gave Iran an opening to pursue a more activist policy in the Middle East.[17] At the same time, implied U.S. threats to pursue regime change in Iran or take military action against the country justified a more energetic Iranian policy at home.[18]

Despite an assertive government and a regional environment conducive to the exercise of Iranian influence, a third factor was required for the development of a more activist Iranian policy: the availability of material resources. The quadrupling of oil prices from 2003 to 2008, a windfall for the Ahmadinejad government, permitted Iran to take a higher profile in the region by allowing it to more freely subsidize such

---

Ithaca Press, 2008, pp. 3–4. Ehteshami and Zweiri note that Ahmadinejad "marks a break in both policy terms and policy outlook" from his predecessors. On the topic of the anti-Israeli rhetoric, see David Menashri, "Iran's Regional Policy: Between Radicalism and Pragmatism," *Journal of International Affairs*, Vol. 60, No. 2, Spring/Summer 2007, p. 5.

[17] A number of developments, in combination, are perceived to have weakened perceptions of U.S. power in the region in ways that could negatively affect U.S. regional interests for years to come. These developments include the United States' challenges in Iraq and Afghanistan; the perceived U.S. failure to bring progress to the Palestinian issue; the increasing influence of Iran and its allies, especially in Lebanon; inconsistencies in the U.S. position on supporting democracy in the region; and the juxtaposition between conditions and events at Abu Ghraib and Guantanamo Bay on the one hand and U.S. moral claims on the other.

[18] For a broad analysis of U.S. policy, see Robert Litwak, *Regime Change: U.S. Strategy Through the Prism of 9/11*, Baltimore, Md.: Johns Hopkins University Press, 2007.

groups as Hezbollah and Hamas.[19] Thus, neither a principlist government nor a changed regional environment by itself is a satisfactory explanation for the shift in Iran's Middle East policy: It is the coincidence of the two, together with new resources, that made the shift possible. Furthermore, the challenges the United States has faced in containing Iran and in effectively managing regional security have arguably made Iran's activism successful (at least temporarily) and, hence, relatively uncontroversial domestically in Iran. However, developments in 2009 have changed these factors in a way that may limit the freedom of any government in Tehran to assert Iranian influence in the Middle East. These developments are (1) a steep drop in oil prices and a global recession that constrains demand and (2) a revamped and nuanced Middle East policy from the new administration in Washington.

Factional Views of Middle East Policy

It is standard among the traditional conservatives (including Khamenei) and the principlists to believe that the United States seeks to dominate the Middle East for the purpose of controlling the region's resources[20] and that the nuclear issue is only an excuse for Washington to pressure Tehran—the real issue, they believe, is Iran's behavior in the region, which the United States seeks to change.[21] The principlist elite also emphasize Iran's new geopolitical standing, which Iranian leaders see as the reason for U.S. pressure on Iran. Critics of the president, such as Larijani and Rezai, agree with Ahmadinejad on this point. According

---

[19] Arguably, the dramatic drop in oil prices will temper Iran's largesse.

[20] For example, see "Iranian Former Guards' Commander Says U.S. Greed Only Problem of Region," Vision of the Islamic Republic of Iran Network 1, February 12, 2008, in BBC Monitoring February 12, 2008; "Iran President Attends Army Day, Pays Tribute to the Armed Forces," Vision of the Islamic Republic of Iran Network 1, April 17, 2008, in BBC Monitoring, April 17, 2008.

[21] See, for example, "Ahmadinezhad Vows Iran Will 'Smash the Face of Any Tyrant,'" Vision of the Islamic Republic of Iran Khuzestan Provincial TV, January 2, 2007, in BBC Monitoring, January 3, 2007; "Resistance Led to Great Nuclear Victory," *Tehran Times*, February 27, 2008; Mahmud Mohammadi, "Eye on Iran" al-Jazeera, January 18, 2008, in "al-Jazeera TV Hosts Discussion on Iranian Nuclear Power Programme," BBC Monitoring, January 26, 2008.

to Larijani, "[the United States] cannot do anything about the geopolitics of Iran so they pursue the military [i.e. nuclear] issue" and "the reason they are so impatient is because Iran has turned into a regional power."[22]

There has also been a palpable sense among principlists that Iran has turned a corner and reached a new stage internationally. Commentators point to "the gradual transfer of power and influence from America's camp to Iran's camp" and see the spread of Islamism in the region going hand in hand with "the inclination of regional states to gravitate toward Iran."[23] The necessary condition for Iran's "advancement" and greater freedom of action, in Larijani's words, is the collapse of the United States' "exclusive hegemony while suffer[ing] a defeat."[24] Shariatmadari concurs that defeating the United States is an integral part of Iran's rise and that the Middle East is now a platform to demonstrate U.S. "failures and disappointments."[25] It is only a short step from this for Ahmadinejad to attribute past Iranian humiliations to the United States and promise to return them in kind.[26] Iran will challenge the United States for the leadership of the region through a "proactive

---

[22] Ali Larijani, "Some in Iran Encourage the West to Issue Resolutions," Fars News Agency Web site, June 19, 2007b; Mohsen Rezai, "Comments on U.S. Pressure," Esfahan Provincial TV, May 11, 2006, in BBC Monitoring, May 13, 2006. One reviewer of a draft of this book noted that that the reasoning expressed here resembles that used by the royalists who maintained that the Shah was toppled because he intended to make Iran a great economic power.

[23] See, respectively, Payman Tajrishi, "Let Us Not Belittle National Achievements," Iran Web site, December 13, 2007, in "Paper Points Out Iran's International Relations Achievements," BBC Monitoring, December 15, 2007a; Hanif Ghaffari, "The Biased Criticism on Foreign Policy," *Resalat* Web site, February 20, 2008, in "Iran Columnist Analyzes Foreign Policy Criticisms by Former Official," BBC Monitoring, February 22, 2008a.

[24] Larijani quoted in A. Savyon, Y. Mansharof, and L. Azuri, "Iran's Attempts to Renew Relations with Egypt," Middle East Media Research Institute, Inquiry and Analysis No. 426, March 12, 2008.

[25] Hoseyn Shariatmadari, "Iran Paper Analyzes Achievements of Revolution," *Kayhan* (Tehran) Web site, April 2, 2008, in BBC Monitoring, April 4, 2008.

[26] Mahmoud Ahmadinejad, Vision of the Islamic Republic of Iran News Network 2, January 2, 2007, in BBC Monitoring, January 3, 2007a.

and aggressive foreign policy" that enables Iran to "play an important role with a minimum of resources and capabilities."[27]

As president, Ahmadinejad has staffed his cabinet with loyalists from the IRGC, members of his family, and other close associates. These appointments have been controversial even in Iran, where personal loyalty often takes precedence over qualifications or competence. A former deputy foreign minister noted that his ministry was humiliated by unparalleled interventions and pressures from "outside" and that experts were replaced by ideologues.[28]

The IRGC, whose leadership is dominated by principlists, has tended to favor Ahmadinejad's approach to the Middle East, focusing on its own exemplary role in resistance and as a vanguard in exporting the revolution in the Islamic world through the "success" of its Qods Force in Lebanon and Iraq. The emphasis on security (as opposed to diplomacy) in Iran's current approach to the Middle East works to the IRGC's advantage and may give the Guards greater weight in policy debates. The IRGC would presumably benefit from this increased visibility by gaining more resources and increasing its prestige; it could also be expected to cash in on new commercial opportunities in the future. Moreover, the government's pronouncements and actions in response to the perceived threat posed by the United States reinforces the IRGC's recent emphasis on "protecting the revolution" from within, an emphasis revealed in its statements supportive of hard-line candidates for the Majles and its deployment of Basiji units to patrol cities and towns in ethnic regions.

Reformist or pragmatic conservative factions that held power during the Rafsanjani and Khatami administrations opposed the principlist school of Middle East and other foreign policy. The reformists and the pragmatic conservatives viewed the principlist government's approach as too provocative, too prone to see the world in zero-sum

---

[27] "A Step Towards Convergence," Resalat Web site, February 21, 2008, in "Iran Paper Praises Government for Re-Establishing Ties with Arabs," BBC Monitoring, February 25, 2008.

[28] Sadeq Kharazzi, "Comments on the Ahmadinejad Government," *E'temad-e Melli* (Tehran) Web site, March 18, 2008, in BBC Monitoring, March 27, 2008.

terms, and blind to areas where U.S.-Iranian interests converged. The reformists and the pragmatic conservatives have tended to be critical of the pro-Ahmadinejad principlists for "confront[ing] the dominant rules of the game" in diplomacy and seeking to establish "relations with nations rather than governments" and, by inference, export the revolution.[29] In contrast, during the reformist period under Khatami, Iran both considered downgrading its ties with Hezbollah to help Tehran reconcile with Washington and sought détente with the Gulf states, two decisions that produced dividends in terms of reaping goodwill toward Iran.[30] An advisor to Khatami during his presidency insisted, years later, that Khatami would not have supported militias or taken sides in the politics of such countries as Lebanon or Iraq and would have supported the rights of the Shi'a, but within the framework of existing states.[31] Traditional and pragmatic conservative critics also tried to outflank Ahmadinejad during his first presidential term, for example by berating him for trying to restore relations with Egypt or for attending a GCC summit conference while Iran was still disputing the issue of ownership of the Tunbs Islands with the UAE.[32]

---

[29] Seyyed Hasan al-Hoseyni, "The Global Mission and a Few Points," *E'temad-e Melli* (Tehran), April 15, 2008, in "Iran Paper Criticizes Ahmadinezhad's Efforts to Change 'World Management,'" BBC Monitoring, April 19, 2008.

[30] See Babak Yektafar, "Under the Thinking Cap: A Conversation with Karim Sadjadpour on U.S.-Iran Relations," *Washington Prism*, February 13, 2008; Abd al-Rahman al-Rashid, "Comments on Iranian Policy Under Khatami," *al-Sharq al-Awsat* (London) Web site, January 7, 2008, in BBC Monitoring, January 8, 2008; Wahid Hashim, comments at "Iran on the Horizon, Panel II: Iran and the Gulf," Middle East Institute Conference Series, Middle East Institute, Washington, D.C., February 1, 2008.

[31] Debate on al-Jazeera TV, January 19, 2008, in BBC Monitoring, January 25, 2008; "Mohammad Shariati, Advisor to Former Iranian President Khatami, Criticizes Ahmadinejad Government over Foreign, Economic Policy and Support for Hizbullah, Iraqi Militias, and Hamas," Middle East Media Research Institute, Special Dispatch No. 1827, January 25, 2008.

[32] *Jomhouri-e Eslami* (Iran), May 21, 2007, quoted in Y. Mansharof, "Dispute in Iran over Renewing Relations with Egypt," Middle East Media Research Institute, Inquiry and Analysis No. 364, June 15, 2007. (*Jomhouri-e Eslami* is reputedly close to Rafsanjani.) On the Gulf, see Sayyed Mohammad Sadr, *E'temad-e Melli* (Tehran) Web site, December 13, 2007, in BBC Monitoring, December 17, 2007.

Among the political heavyweights in Iran, one of the most experienced and most voluble critics is Rowhani, a pragmatic conservative who often accuses the president of excessively provocative rhetoric that works against Iran's interests and, indeed, endangers the revolution and the republic.[33] Rafsanjani, a leading pragmatic conservative who has criticized Ahmadinejad's "adventurism," seeks to reassure the West that Iran does not seek to dominate the region "or to interfere in other countries' spheres of influence" but simply wants to improve "cooperation with other states."[34] Rather than focus on the rivalry between the United States and Iran, Rafsanjani highlights common interests in Iraq: "Iran needs a peaceful, independent, free, Muslim and democratic neighbor today, and this is what the Iraqi people want, too."[35] He does not deny Iran's support for oppressed people and desire for the U.S. withdrawal from Iraq; he simply does not see these issues as either paramount or necessarily resulting in unremitting hostility between Iran and the United States. Qalibaf, a "moderate" principlist, takes a similar tack, stressing the "fact that Iran and the U.S. have many common interests in the region; . . . [Iran's] position in the region should not be one of opposition, but friendly competition with other powers."[36]

These opposing views over Iran's foreign policy in Middle East (and, by extension, U.S.-Iranian interaction in the region) have been manifested in factional competition and intra-elite rivalry, which, in turn, have affected Iran's relations with the region and with the United States. A notable example of behind-the-scenes competition emerged in early 2002 following the overthrow of the Taliban in Afghanistan. Under the Khatami administration, Iran was cooperating with U.S.-led international efforts in Bonn to form a successor regime in Kabul. By all accounts, this cooperation was critical to the success of these

---

[33] Ali Akbar Dareini, "Iran's Ex-Nuke Negotiator Slams Ahmadinejad's Nuclear, Foreign Strategy," Associated Press, February 27, 2008.

[34] Akbar Hashemi Rafsanjani, quoted by Mehr News Agency, February 12, 2008, in BBC Monitoring, February 13, 2008a; Akbar Hashemi Rafsanjani, quoted in Voice of the Islamic Republic of Iran, April 11, 2008, in BBC Monitoring, April 14, 2008b.

[35] Rafsanjani, 2008a; Rafsanjani, 2008b.

[36] "A Rival for Iran's Ahmadinejad," *Time Magazine*, March 18, 2008.

efforts. Moreover, Iranian diplomats expressed interest in cooperating with the United States on issues other than Afghanistan, and a breakthrough in U.S.-Iranian relations appeared possible.

Then, in January 2002, Israeli vessels in the Red Sea captured the *Karine-A*, a merchant ship loaded with 50 tons of weapons destined for the Palestinian Authority. It was discovered that the purchase of the weapons had been funded by Hezbollah and that the weapons had been loaded onto the ship on Iran's Kish Island. Days later, Iran was added to the "axis of evil" in George W. Bush's State of the Union address.[37] Ansari noted with suspicion that it was "remarkable that a regime hitherto experienced in shipping arms and munitions overseas should choose to do this particular delivery via slow boat journey around the Arabian Peninsula."[38] James Dobbins, the U.S. representative to the Bonn talks, recounted his conversation with one Iranian diplomat soon after the incident. The Iranian told Dobbins that Khatami had asked the representatives on the SNSC if they had known about the shipment on the *Karine-A*, and all denied knowledge. The diplomat then asked Dobbins if the U.S. government had contradictory information.[39] The *Karine-A* incident appears to be a clear example of a faction in the Iranian elite—one whose interest lay in U.S.-Iranian confrontation in the region—undermining a policy defined by a competing faction. Given the Supreme Leader's perceived distrust of the United States, one could speculate that Khamenei had prior knowledge of the shipment or even that he instigated the crisis in an effort to forestall a potential imbalance among factions.

Another example of factional and personal competition in shaping Iran's policy toward the Middle East arose after the capture by IRGC

---

[37] See Gary Sick, "Iran: Confronting Terrorism," *Washington Quarterly*, Vol. 26, No. 4, Autumn 2003, p. 90; U.S. House of Representatives, "Recognizing Iran as a Strategic Threat: An Intelligence Challenge for the United States," Staff Report of the House Permanent Select Committee on Intelligence, Subcommittee on Intelligence Policy, Washington, D.C., August 23, 2003, p. 20; and Geoffrey Kemp, "U.S. and Iran: The Nuclear Dilemma: Next Steps," The Nixon Center, Washington, D.C., April 2004, p. 8.

[38] Ali M. Ansari, "Iran and the U.S. in the Shadow of 9/11: Persia and the Persian Question Revisited," *Iranian Studies*, Vol. 39, No. 2, June 2006, p. 164.

[39] Dobbins in Green et al., 2009, p. 68.

naval elements of 15 British sailors and marines from the HMS *Cornwall* in the Persian Gulf in March 2007. This incident occurred in the context of an ongoing debate among the Iranian elite—in particular, among principlists and between them and pragmatic conservatives—over the appropriate level of Ahmadinejad's control of foreign policy and the degree of confrontation with the West that Iran should be willing to pursue. The president appeared to favor prolonging the crisis to gain advantage in this debate, but his national security adviser at the time, Larijani, began talks with the British government. These talks, which seemed to undermine Ahmadinejad's efforts, prompted the president to pay a highly publicized visit to the detainees and award a medal to the IRGC commander who ordered the seizure.[40] When the captives were suddenly released, Ahmadinejad "pardoned" them, a prerogative he does not legally enjoy as president of the Islamic Republic.[41] A great deal of factional parrying went on both during and after the crisis, with principlists hailing a strong and compassionate Iran that could "humiliate" a "weak" United Kingdom and pragmatic conservatives accusing the government of "weakness" in the face of a supposed "effective threat" against Iran by then–Prime Minister Tony Blair.[42]

Numerous other examples of factional competition in shaping Iran's policy toward the Middle East can be found, and each has origins in factions' efforts to improve their domestic positions vis-à-vis other groups. Despite broad Iranian public support for Hezbollah in its 2006 confrontation with Israel, reformists questioned whether the financial support Tehran provided Hezbollah and other foreign movements was adding to the Iranian people's economic deprivation—

[40] Adam Goodman, "Iran: Informal Networks and Leadership Politics," Advanced Research and Assessment Group, Defence Academy of the United Kingdom, Middle East Series No. 08/12, April 2008, p. 16.

[41] Ansari, 2007, p. 79.

[42] *Aftabnews* (Tehran) Web site, April 4, 2007, in "OSC Analysis: Iran—Domestic Media Praise, Criticize Government's Handling of Crisis with Britain," Dialog/World News Connection 0242201037, April 6, 2007a; Rajanews Web site, April 4, 2007, in "OSC Analysis: Iran—Domestic Media Praise, Criticize Government's Handling of Crisis with Britain," Dialog/World News Connection 0242201037, April 6, 2007.

deprivation that had not diminished despite then-high oil prices.[43] Editorials in *Kayhan* in 2007 by Shariatmadari, the paper's editor in chief (and Khamenei's special representative) advocating Iran's historic claim to Bahrain prompted Mottaki to travel to Manama to apologize, and they also led reformists to criticize the editorial as a "drunken ballad" that would cause "disruption and confrontation" in the region.[44] Even Ahmadinejad's strident calls for the elimination of Israel have prompted criticism from factional opponents who deride such rhetoric as potentially leading to a destructive confrontation with the United States.[45]

Summary: Leadership Dynamics and Iranian Middle East Policy

In sum, Iranian policymaking vis-à-vis the Middle East certainly has been affected by momentous changes in the regional security environment facing the Islamic Republic. However, factional maneuvering also plays a major role in how Iran portrays itself to the region and drives what is arguably a strategically incoherent policy approach to the Middle East. Factions and key individuals associated with them use Middle East and other foreign policies as a tool to improve their own domestic positions and weaken their rivals. The prevalence of factional rivalry in Iranian leadership dynamics creates a government "unable to articulate a coherent strategic vision and whose frequently erratic and escalatory behavior may be serving the parochial goals of key elites rather than the state's larger interests."[46]

However, the degree of factional and personal competition evident in Iranian policymaking vis-à-vis the Middle East does not approach the level evident in Iranian policymaking vis-à-vis both the

---

[43] See, for example, Shaaki.blogfa.com, "Yek Chah Baray e Takhlih e Ravani [A Well for Mental Offloading]," December 31, 2006.

[44] *Kargozaran* (Tehran), July 18, 2007, in "OSC Analysis: Revival of Claim to Bahrain Sparks Media Debate," Dialog/World News Connection 0247601137, July 23, 2007. The Bahrain incident is indicative of Iranian diplomatic ineptitude, which, in the past, has earned Iran unwarranted enemies. The incident also demonstrates Iran's strong streak of anti-Arab arrogance, which is immediately sensed by Iran's neighbors.

[45] Sammy Salama and Gina Cabrera Farraj, "Top Iranian Political Figures Divided Over Nuclear Program," *WMD Insights*, June 2006.

[46] Wehrey, Thaler, et al., 2009, p. 23.

nuclear program and the government's interaction with the international community. We turn now to factionalism as a determinant of Iranian nuclear policy.

The Nuclear Case: Factionalism, Personality, and Policymaking

The nuclear program has arguably become one of the most pressing issues shaping Iranian factional politics. It illustrates the policy fissures both between the principlist and reformist/pragmatic conservative camps and within the principlist camp itself. Additionally, it demonstrates that the Supreme Leader must undertake a certain level of factional balancing even in the context of a core national-security interest. In this section, we examine the interplay between factionalism, personality, and policy with respect to the nuclear issue between 2003 and 2009.

This length of time can be conveniently divided in two pieces: the Khatami period (2003–2005) and the Ahmadinejad period (2005–present), which differ in a number of ways. The earlier period coincided with the height of U.S. power and confidence (and Iranian caution), and the later period coincided with the U.S. preoccupation with Iraq and Iran's renewed confidence. During the first period, a reformist government responded to the nuclear crisis by embracing diplomacy and engagement with the United States (particularly on the topic of Afghanistan) but found itself, as time went by, under fire from domestic critics who demanded that Iran make fewer concessions and take a tougher stand. During the second period, a principlist government, suspicious of diplomacy, adopted a policy of resistance by largely ignoring the UN Security Council and its resolutions. The nuclear question was increasingly appropriated by pro-Ahmadinejad principlists for domestic, partisan advantage. The previous Iranian nuclear negotiators were accused of retreat and compromise (especially by such critics as Larijani), and Ahmadinejad attributed the UN Security Council's failure to stop Iran's enrichment program to his own administration's steadfastness. The U.S. National Intelligence Estimate (NIE) in December 2007 appeared to reduce the likelihood of a U.S. military attack on Iran, thereby weakening Ahmadinejad's reformist/ pragmatic conservative critics and perhaps vindicating the principlist line on nuclear negotiations that Ahmadinejad had adopted.

Shifts in Iran's policy on the nuclear issue reflect both changing assessments of Iran's overall interests and disagreements about negotiations and the proper functions of diplomacy. How the issue has been defined, how policy has changed, and how some are blamed and others are credited with success tell us something about the role of personalities and opportunism—as well as principle—in defining policy. Iranian policies surrounding the nuclear program have been the test of two different approaches to a critical national issue.

The Reformist Approach: Building Confidence Abroad, Losing Ground at Home

The extent of Iran's nuclear ambitions surfaced during the Khatami administration, when revelations about undeclared sites emerged in mid-2002. Once these sites, and the facility at Natanz in particular, were made public, there was a clear risk that the IAEA Board of Governors would refer the matter to the UN Security Council, where the issue would become political rather than technical. At the same time, Iran felt extreme pressure from the increased U.S. presence in the region, from its perception that an attack on Iraq was imminent, and from its fears that the United States might find an excuse to attack Iran next. Less than a year after the 2001 al-Qaeda attacks on the United States, Iran was anxious not to do anything to provoke an already enraged United States into military action. Thus, the disclosure of Iran's nuclear program in mid-2002 could not have come at a worse time, from the Iranian perspective. The Iranian regime may have interpreted the disclosure as a direct threat against the government, and this, in turn, may have brought about the (rare and temporary) interfactional consensus on the proper response. It seems, as the 2007 NIE suggests, that the government took measures to reduce the perceived threat to the regime by ending the weapons element of the program in 2003 and adopting a conciliatory approach diplomatically.[47]

The nuclear dossier was immediately entrusted by Khamenei to the pragmatic conservative Rowhani, the secretary of the SNSC, and a team of negotiators and assistants was assigned to him. From the outset, Rowhani's aim was to defuse the crisis and prevent the issue from being sent to the UN Security Council. Initial soundings showed him that, to escape censure or worse, Iran needed to reassure the international community of the peaceful intent behind the nuclear program. To this end, Iran agreed, in the Sa'dabad Declaration in Autumn 2003, to subject its program to the Additional Protocol to the Nuclear Non-Proliferation Treaty, a set of inspections more intrusive than those previously in force, and to suspend its enrichment activities. A year later, in Paris, Iran made a similar agreement with the three principal European Union (EU) states (Great Britain, France, and Germany, known as the EU3). Iran took pains to stress that this suspension was temporary and voluntary, and that Iran itself would terminate it. Rowhani wanted to show Iran's flexibility and thus rebuild trust and confidence with the international community. He argued that acceptance of the suspension was necessary to "remove any excuses that America might have"[48] to attack Iran. Because the suspension was voluntary and circumscribed, it did not interfere with the expansion of Iran's peaceful nuclear program. As Rowhani argued, "On the one hand we negotiated our way through the danger and on the other hand, we successfully completed our technology and know-how."[49]

However, because the Majles elections of 2004 introduced new Majles members—including many deputies with IRGC backgrounds—who made the institution more conservative, criticism from opposing

---

[47] For background, see the sources cited in Shahram Chubin, 2006. See also Chubin in Tellis and Wills, 2007.

[48] For the sources cited in the text, see Rowhani, 2008b; *Tehran-e Emrooz* (Tehran), December 13, 2007, in BBC Monitoring, December 15, 2007b; Mehr News Agency, December 20, 2007, in BBC Monitoring, December 12, 2007c.

[49] For the sources cited in the text, see Rowhani, 2008b; *Tehran-e Emrooz* (Tehran), 2007b; Mehr News Agency, 2007c.

factions increased. The principlists likened the Paris agreement to swapping a pearl for a lollipop,[50] suggesting that the constraints on enrichment that Iran accepted were too onerous and that Iran was receiving virtually nothing in return. Both Rowhani's discussions with the EU3 and the three countries' demands that Iran limit and reverse centrifuge production seemed less acceptable the more the shadow of serious military consequences receded (i.e., the more U.S. military forces were perceived to be in a "quagmire" in Iraq). By June 2005 and Ahmadinejad's election as president (an election that had more to do with the reformists' domestic failings than with foreign policy), Iran's negotiations with the EU3 had stalled. The Iranian negotiators—looking over their shoulders at Tehran—were less and less accommodating, and their bargaining tactics frustrated their EU3 colleagues. Even before a new team of negotiators replaced the Iranian delegation, the old team had categorically rejected the incentive package (which an influential newspaper called "a bubble and illusion"[51]) the EU3 had offered in mid-2005. Ahmadinejad later ridiculed the incentive package:

> [Y]ou [Iran] should give up enrichment and any fuel production forever and in return we [the West] will send you our people to train you on using the internet, and will let you trade with us, and if a nuclear country attacks you, we will let you complain to the Security Council.[52]

The Principlist Approach: Maintaining "Steadfastness"

After 2005, Iran largely dispensed with diplomacy, preferring to create faits accomplis on the technology side while stalling on the diplomatic front. This principlist approach reflected a belief that diplomacy was a losing game, with the odds stacked in favor of the United States (in the UN Security Council or elsewhere), and that power counted for more

---

[50] A phrase attributed to Ali Larijani. See Ali Larijani, quoted in "We Gave Pearl and Received Bonbon in Exchange," Fars News Agency, November 15, 2004, in "Iranian Daily Says Supreme Leader's Rep Has Reservations About Paris Nuclear Talks," Dialog/World News Connection 0198550647, November 15, 2004.

[51] *Kayhan* (Tehran) Web site, December 3, 2007, in BBC Monitoring, December 5, 2007.

[52] Iran TV Channel 1, February 23, 2008, in BBC Monitoring, February 25, 2008.

than words. As with Iran's Middle East policy, this approach found its expression in the catchphrases "resistance" and "steadfastness," which implied determination to fight "bullies" and secure Iran's "rights." The new approach to the nuclear issue had both an international and a domestic side. Internationally, it was characterized by a refusal to accept the limits agreed upon earlier and by a determination to restart the enrichment and centrifuge programs. After 2005, Iran's principlist government refused to take the threat of the IAEA referral to the UN Security Council as seriously as its reformist predecessors had and thus found itself in that chamber by the end of 2006. Its strategy was to retaliate against UN resolutions and future sanctions by threatening to cease and then actually limiting its cooperation with the IAEA, notably with IAEA inspectors.

Domestically, the nuclear issue evolved into a matter of factional rivalry *and* state legitimacy. Under the principlists, the nuclear program became a bellwether of Iranian independence and a demonstration of national pride and technological know-how. This evolution of the nuclear issue also made it paramount for Iran not to look weak, especially in negotiations, and it allowed the government to paint its reformist and pragmatic conservative critics as working against the interests of the Islamic Republic. Moreover, Ahmadinejad took what had been largely an elite issue and made it a popular one by elevating it to a matter of basic principle. By repeatedly discussing the issue—in his more than 30 trips to the provinces—as one of nuclear rights and the West's attempts to deny them to Iran, he played on the favorite narrative of Iran's victimhood and the need for resistance. Ahmadinejad lashed out at his predecessors—now his critics—as cowards and, even worse, traitors, accusing them of giving comfort to the enemy through their dissent and their exaggeration of the dangers of sanctions.[53] He painted them as people "asking for America's permission to progress."[54] At the

---

[53] For an example, see Mahmoud Ahmadinejad, Islamic Republic News Agency Web site, February 11, 2008, in BBC Monitoring, February 12, 2008a. For commentary, see *Mardom Salari* (Tehran) Web site, November 28, 2007, in BBC Monitoring, December 1, 2007. See also Ansari, 2007, p. 50

[54] Voice of the Islamic Republic of Iran, February 17, 2008, in BBC Monitoring, February 18, 2008.

same time, he claimed that the nuclear issue had "enhanced national unity" and increased Iran's prestige.[55] He did not claim sole authorship of this perceived success but attributed it to the "steadfastness" of the Supreme Leader: "the world has to know that Ahmadinejad is one member of this great nation and only expresses the stance of Iran and the Supreme Leader."[56] Ahmadinejad's novel mobilization of the populace in the largely neglected rural areas behind the slogan of securing Iran's rights made reasonable discourse among the Iranian elite both harder and, when there was discourse, more extreme.[57]

Factionalism and Personal Rivalry Deepen Under Ahmadinejad

Ahmadinejad's rhetoric and open defiance of the United States were, however, arguably endangering the Islamic Republic by making a U.S. military attack on Iran an increasingly real possibility. In fact, in early 2007, after Ahmadinejad contended in a television interview that the Americans were "engaged only in psychological warfare" and were "incapable" of harming the Islamic Republic, his critics harshly attacked him for complacency over a potential U.S. strike on Iran.[58] His principlist supporters joined him in denigrating the U.S. threat as "empty talk" whose goal was to "push us into giving up our resistance."[59] Opponents, particularly pragmatic conservatives and anti-Ahmadinejad principlists, rejected the government's diminution of

---

[55] Mahmoud Ahmadinejad, "Speech to Supreme Leader," Vision of the Islamic Republic of Iran Network 1, July 2, 2007, in BBC Monitoring, July 3, 2007c. Earlier, a supportive newspaper referred to the unity that came from "nuclear nationalism." See *Jomhouri-e Eslami* (Iran), August 20, 2006, in BBC Monitoring, August 30, 2006.

[56] Mahmoud Ahmadinejad, Vision of the Islamic Republic of Iran Network 1, February 11, 2008, in BBC Monitoring, February 13, 2008b.

[57] For more on the principlist approach to the nuclear issue and the role of public opinion, see Green, Wehrey, and Wolf, 2009, pp. 28–33, 52–65; Chubin, 2006; Chubin, 2007.

[58] Mahmoud Ahmadinejad, interview with Vision of the Islamic Republic of Iran Network 2, January 23, 2007, in "Critics Berate Ahmadinezhad for Complacency over Threats to Iran," Dialog/World News Connection 0238750465, January 27, 2007b.

[59] *Kayhan* (Tehran), April 3, 2007, in "OSC Analysis: Iran: Hardliners Play Down Opponents' Warnings of U.S. Military Strike," Dialog/World News Connection 0242801514, April 18, 2007.

the threat of U.S. attack. Expediency Council Secretary Rezai, former commander of the IRGC, suggested that U.S. forces could attack Iran's nuclear facilities with missiles, and a Rafsanjani-associated Web site stated that "worries about U.S. military action are real."[60] Reportedly, a group of 100 Majles deputies asked Rafsanjani, as head of the Expediency Council, to intervene in the government's confrontational handling of the nuclear issue.[61] Khamenei appears to have played both sides of the debate, warning Iranian politicians and journalists "not to advance the enemy's objectives" by "fostering the mistrust of officials and the government"[62] on one hand and reportedly emphasizing that the "threats are serious"[63] on the other.

The severity of the factional debate over the nuclear issue may have reached its apex in November 2007, when Ahmadinejad began referring to his critics as traitors, a very serious allegation with potentially grave consequences. This attack was followed by an MOIS announcement that charges of espionage had been brought against Hossein Musavian, a senior nuclear negotiator who had served under Khatami's chief negotiator, Rowhani. Both Rowhani and Musavian had been vociferous critics of the government's approach to the nuclear issue.[64] Two weeks after the announcement, the judiciary cleared Musavian of espionage charges; even then, however, Ahmadinejad supporters derided perceived pressures on the judiciary from Musavian's backers among senior officials of the Expediency Council, a likely reference to Rafsanjani and Rezai.

---

[60] *Aftabnews* (Tehran) Web site, April 6, 2007, in "OSC Analysis: Iran: Hardliners Play Down Opponents' Warnings of U.S. Military Strike," Dialog/World News Connection 0242801514, April 18, 2007b.

[61] *Aftab-e Yazd* (Tehran) Web site, January 25, 2007, in "Critics Berate Ahmadinezhad for Complacency over Threats to Iran," Dialog/World News Connection 0238750465, January 27, 2007a.

[62] Khamenei's *nowrooz* [new year] message on the Supreme Leader's Web site as reported in *Aftabnews* (Tehran) Web site, 2007b.

[63] Related by Rafsanjani during a meeting with 100 Majles deputies (Baztab, January 24, 2007, in "OSC Analysis: Critics Berate Ahmadinezhad for Complacency over Threats to Iran," Dialog/World News Connection 0238750465, January 27, 2007).

[64] See Breffni O'Rourke, "Iran: Ahmadinejad's Threat to 'Traitors' Points to Widening Rift," Radio Free Europe/Radio Liberty, November 14, 2007.

The publication of the U.S. NIE in December 2007 alleviated much of the pressure on Ahmadinejad by weakening the arguments of his critics and perhaps even vindicating his radical approach. By focusing on Iran's cessation of the weaponization of the nuclear program in 2003, the NIE made a U.S. military option against Iran less defensible in the United States. The NIE also undermined Iranian reformists and pragmatic conservatives who advocated compromise and moderation on the nuclear issue.[65] Ahmadinejad portrayed the NIE as "the greatest victory of the Iranian people in the past 100 years," calling it a "clear shift of policies."[66] He also claimed that the victory of the Iranian people came from the U.S. acceptance of a "nuclear Iran" and said that only "with the grace of God and the wisdom of the Supreme Leader all has ended in Iran's favor."[67] The president was justified in claiming success:

> It is nearly two and a half years since we began serious resistance [to opponents of the nuclear program]. Not only have we not made any [new] concessions but we have abandoned past commitments that were onerous and destructive.[68]

The nuclear case clearly demonstrates the prevalence of factional competition, where domestic priorities and rivalries overlap with and affect Iran's most important national-security debates. But, even within factions, personal rivalry and ambition can also affect the coherence of policymaking on major issues. Larijani provides a case in point.

Larijani, whom Ahmadinejad had ousted from his position as chief nuclear negotiator in 2007, shared in Ahmadinejad's gloat-

---

[65] See Najmeh Bozorgmehr and Roula Khalaf, "Dismay as Top Nuclear Official Quits," *Financial Times* (London), October 22, 2007a, p. 2; Kaveh Afriasabi and Kayhan Bozorgmehr, "The View from Iran," *The Boston Globe*, December 5, 2007.

[66] "Where Is This All Going?" 2007.

[67] Mehr News Agency, December 5, 2007, in BBC Monitoring, December 6, 2007b.

[68] Quoted in Najmeh Bozorgmehr, "President Hostage to His Promises," *Financial Times* (London), February 28, 2008a. At the very least, the hardliners could argue that the quality of proposals from the West had improved. See *Kayhan* (Tehran) Web site, 2007.

ing over the 2007 NIE: "This is a great fiasco for the Americans."[69] One of the most vocal critics of the moderate approach to the nuclear question under Rowhani, Larijani was chosen by the Supreme Leader to replace him. Larijani had run against Ahmadinejad for the presidency in 2005 and would not have been Ahmadinejad's first choice to replace Rowhani, but exploiting such rivalries is consistent with the Supreme Leader's tendency to keep as many elements in play as he can, the better to balance them and to maneuver among them. Contemptuous of Ahmadinejad,[70] Larijani accepted the assignment, perhaps with the understanding that he would lead the nuclear negotiations. Given his association with the IRGC and the support he received from senior clerics, Larijani assumed that his relationship with Ahmadinejad would be similar to the one between Rowhani and Khatami: one of trust and delegation. Larijani soon found himself on a short leash, however, with Ahmadinejad making policy with a small circle of close advisors outside the SNSC.[71] When Larijani was not publicly contradicted by the president, he was routinely marginalized from decisionmaking.[72] Larijani's response was to state that the judgments of the SNSC are

---

[69] Vision of the Islamic Republic of Iran Network 2, December 4, 2007, in BBC Monitoring, December 5, 2007.

[70] Ansari, 2007, p. 50.

[71] See *Aftab-e Yazd* (Tehran) Web site, October 21, 2007, in BBC Monitoring, October 24, 2007b.

[72] Despite severely criticizing Rowhani's diplomatic approach to the nuclear issue, Larijani adopted a similar diplomatic approach to the nuclear negotiations. He found discussions with Xavier Solana, the EU's foreign-policy chief, to be a useful way to defuse U.S. and UN Security Council pressures (even to the point of returning to the subject of a "double freeze" in mid-2007). Thus, Larijani viewed agreement with the Europeans as not necessarily entailing surrender or submission. Unfortunately for Larijani, Ahmadinejad had not witnessed a parallel evolution. This rendered Larijani's frequent meetings with Solana mostly unproductive. In addition, when he agreed to a timetable for discussions and for resolution of outstanding issues with Solana and the IAEA, Larijani found himself repudiated by Ahmadinejad, who publicly remarked that the nuclear case was "closed." See Bozorgmehr and Khalaf, 2007a; Sasan Aga'i, "Why Larijani Left," *E'temad-e Melli* (Tehran), October 24, 2007, in BBC Monitoring, October 26, 2007. The word "closed" recurred in early 2008, when Ahmadinejad repeated that, to all intents and purposes, the case was closed and Iran would only discuss residual issues with the IAEA (i.e., *not* with the Europeans or the UN Security Council). See Iran TV Channel 1, 2008.

the authoritative expression of foreign policy and that Ahmadinejad was merely expressing his own view.[73] It may have been Ahmadinejad's insistence on personally controlling the "nuclear dossier" (though with the Supreme Leader retaining ultimate decisionmaking authority) that led to Larijani's forced resignation in October 2007.[74]

Following Larijani's resignation, Khamenei's foreign-affairs advisor, Velayati, perhaps speaking on the Supreme Leader's behalf, suggested that it would have been "better" if the resignation had not occurred.[75] Khamenei appointed Larijani as his personal representative in the SNSC, in addition to Rowhani, thereby ensuring that Larijani, an important personality, remained in the fold. Ahmadinejad may then have prevailed on Khamenei to nominate the president's own personal confidante, Jalili, as the next secretary of the SNSC and chief nuclear negotiator. Lest there were doubts about nuclear policy, Jalili told his European interlocutors that Larijani's proposals were void and that any future discussions would have to start at zero.[76] Notably, despite the president's insistence that the nuclear case was "closed," Rafsanjani had reiterated that Iran is prepared to negotiate with the United States, but without preconditions (i.e., without Iran suspending its enrichment program).[77]

Larijani's dispute with Ahmadinejad reveals that there are fissures between personal rivals even within the principlist faction, which has been, more often than not, united on national security issues. It also highlights the Supreme Leader's efforts to ensure that key personalities remain in the fold. Since being elected speaker of the Majles in spring 2008, Larijani has reentered the arena of nuclear policymaking and appears to be trying to outflank Ahmadinejad on the nuclear issue by

---

[73] Ali Larijani, "Interview," *Aftab-e Yazd* (Tehran) Web site, October 21, 2007, in BBC Monitoring, October 24, 2007c.

[74] For an in-depth examination of Larijani's resignation, see Posch, 2007.

[75] Ali Akbar Velayati, interview with Iranian Student's News Agency, October 22, 2007.

[76] See Elaine Sciolino, "Iran Pushes Nuclear Talks Back to Zero," *The New York Times*, December 2, 2007.

[77] Friday Sermon, Voice of the Islamic Republic of Iran, March 14, 2008, in BBC Monitoring, March 17, 2008.

increasing the visibility and stature of the Majles in Iran's relationship with the IAEA.[78] Whether he has been given leeway by the Supreme Leader to affect the substance of nuclear policy is unclear. So far, Ahmadinejad may believe that his policy of continuing the nuclear program without interruption may have paid off, especially in light of Obama's gestures toward Iran and U.S. willingness to participate fully in multilateral discussions over the nuclear issue.

Khamenei's Factional Preferences Regarding the Nuclear Issue

Khamenei, as we have seen, has the last word on every major issue affecting the Islamic Republic. He is the ultimate authority on security issues insofar as he is commander in chief and all the security services and the entire military are directly answerable to him. Foreign and security policy have been a daily preoccupation of the Islamic Republic since its inception, with crises succeeding war in rapid succession. As a revolutionary state, Iran considers foreign policy particularly important and sees it an expression of the country's vitality and continued influence. Khamenei came into his position with no special qualifications: He is neither well-traveled or worldly, like Rafsanjani, nor curious, like Khatami.

Although Khamenei may not be knowledgeable about the details of the nuclear issue, he has nevertheless expressed strong opinions about it. He may see the international effort to stop the nuclear program as an attempt by the West to keep Iran from developing scientific knowledge and technology (and self-sufficiency in both), with Western allegations that Iran is pursuing nuclear weapons being merely an excuse to deny Iran the technology necessary for civilian development.[79]

Iran's policy on the nuclear issue, especially under the principlists, has reflected Khamenei's views. Kazem Jalali, a Majles deputy, has observed that the Supreme Leader "is the main arbitrator of the

---

[78] When the May 2008 IAEA report was released, Larijani distanced himself from the Iranian government's positive review of the report by calling the document "deplorable" and promising that the Majles would get involved in evaluating Iran's "future behavior with the IAEA" (Hoseyni, 2008).

[79] Sadjadpour, 2008, pp. 22–24.

different levels of the nuclear policy."[80] Jalili, after his appointment as secretary of the SNSC, noted that Iran's nuclear policy is clear: "Both Mr. Larijani and I only follow the government's policies"; hence, nuclear policy does not depend on individuals but reflects a "national consensus."[81] The ability to attribute decisions to a consensus may in fact be a safety net that the SNSC provides to the Iranian system: All are responsible, and no one, especially the Supreme Leader, will have to take the blame if things go awry. An influential journalist echoed this view, arguing that it is meaningless to talk of "strategic differences of opinion" between the president and the former secretary of the SNSC, Larijani, since they only execute decisions made by the Supreme Leader.[82] Ahmadinejad has thanked the Supreme Leader for his instructions "in foreign policy, too, regarding which your eminence follows every detail every day and offers guidance."[83] A less modest role is ascribed to the president by his intimate, Mojtaba Samareh-Hashemi: "The country's nuclear policy is determined and declared by the Supreme Leader, Ayatollah Ali Khamenei, *and President Ahmadinejad*."[84]

The Supreme Leader appears to share the principlist world view—distrust of Western intentions and the need for Iran to assert itself internationally—and believes that a passive strategy is not sufficient to meet the U.S. threat. Both Khamenei and Ahmadinejad also believe

---

[80] Rapporteur of the Majles' Council on Security, Iran TV, October 23, 2007, in BBC Monitoring, October 24, 2007.

[81] Sa'id Jalili, Islamic Republic of Iran News Network, November 15, 2007, in BBC Monitoring, November 17, 2007. This sentiment was echoed by Larijani: "Different government's [sic] adopt different tactics, but they all function under [the] auspices of the Supreme Leader and they have all pursued the same path so far" (Iranian Student's News Agency Web site, December 10, 2007, in BBC Monitoring, December 13, 2007a).

[82] Hoseyn Shariatmadari, "Comments on Influence of the Supreme Leader," *Kayhan* (Tehran) Web site, October 22, 2007, in BBC Monitoring, October 24, 2007.

[83] Vision of the Islamic Republic of Iran Network 1, August 27, 2007, in BBC Monitoring, August 30, 2007 (emphasis added).

[84] Islamic Republic News Agency Web site, October 20, 2007, in BBC Monitoring, October 22, 2007 (emphasis added). Conversely, note the following criticism of the president's tendency to claim credit for the nuclear policy: "He is only part of a committee" and is "under the supervision of the Supreme Leader" (*E'temad-e Melli* [Tehran], December 10, 2007, in BBC Monitoring, December 12, 2007).

that Iran should have a more important role regionally.[85] The result is that Khamenei has given Ahmadinejad plenty of leeway to conduct foreign policy, from the president's rambling letters to foreign heads of state (including George W. Bush, German Chancellor Angela Merkel, French President Nicolas Sarkozy, and the Pope) to controversial visits to the UN General Assembly in New York. Ahmadinejad has ridiculed those who believe that there are differences between him and the Supreme Leader on the nuclear issue, saying that he and Khamenei, when together, "only laugh at their ignorance."[86] It is certainly true that the Supreme Leader has singled out Ahmadinejad and his policies for praise much more often and more sincerely than he did Khatami and his policies.[87] Khamenei's special relationship with Ahmadinejad even extended to support for the president in the March 2008 Majles elections. And in the run-up to the 2009 presidential elections, the Supreme Leader implied his preference for Ahmadinejad by deriding the other three candidates' advocacy of better relations with the West as "a disaster for the Iranian nation."[88] Khamenei has told the Assembly of Experts that Ahmadinejad's role in and resistance against the West on the nuclear issue was very "conspicuous" in the final victory over the West, and he has depicted Ahmadinejad's critics (including some members of the previous administration) as the instruments of foreigners.[89]

---

[85] For one popular source on this, see "Iran: They Think They Have Right on Their Side," *Economist*, November 24, 2007, pp. 47–49.

[86] Najmeh Bozorgmehr, "Khamene'i Urged to Rein in President," *Financial Times* (London), November 13, 2007.

[87] Indeed, one conservative source claimed that such praise of a government "has been almost unprecedented" (Hamid Omidi, *Kayhan* [Tehran] Web site, September 22, 2007, in BBC Monitoring, September 24, 2007).

[88] Ali Khamenei, speech in Kordestan, Islamic Republic of Iran News Network TV, in "Iran: Supreme Leader Urges Nation Not to Vote for Those 'Who Submit' to Enemies," Dialog/World News Connection 0280851456, May 19, 2009.

[89] "Resistance Led to Great Nuclear Victory," 2008; Islamic Republic News Agency Web site, February 26, 2008, in BBC Monitoring, February 27, 2008; Daniel Dombey and Harvey Morris, "U.S. Sees Tehran Nuclear Dispute Going into 2009," *Financial Times* (London), February 27, 2008.

Khamenei went even further in the March 2008 Majles elections, putting his own prestige behind Ahmadinejad, praising the incumbent assembly for supporting the nuclear program (while noting that certain elements in the previous Majles had tried to dissuade the country from pursuing nuclear technology), and suggesting that the people should avoid voting for what he characterized as U.S.-backed Majles candidates, implicitly referring to reformist candidates. Finally, recognizing that domestic issues were uppermost in the minds of the electorate, he tied Ahmadinejad's sterling performance on the nuclear issue to Iran's economic ills by concluding that the government is "doing its best to render services to the nation."[90]

Khamenei has also gone beyond merely praising Ahmadinejad's approach on nuclear policy: The Supreme Leader actually claims ownership of the approach. He revealed that it was his own direct intervention in mid-2005, just before Ahmadinejad's election, that stopped a course of "retreat" under the previous government:

> I said the course of retreating must come to an end and turn into a course of advancing. Moreover, I said that the first step must be taken by the same government which had begun the process of retreating. And this did happen . . . . It was decided to resume the work on the Esfahan UFC [uranium-conversion facility].[91]

Praising Ahmadinejad (and his nuclear stance) and intervening in the 2009 presidential election on his behalf were not without danger. In doing so, the Supreme Leader assumed that the risks associated with the nuclear issue had decreased, the tide having turned with the publication of the 2007 NIE. He also assumed that the political capital the government had built by emphasizing the nuclear issue would impel the Iranian public to overlook the absence of performance on the economic front. Praising and supporting Ahmadinejad put the Supreme Leader clearly on the principlist side of the political spectrum. In

---

[90] Vision of the Islamic Republic of Iran Network 1, March 12, 2008, in BBC Monitoring, March 13, 2008b.

[91] Vision of the Islamic Republic of Iran Network 1, January 3, 2008, in BBC Monitoring, January 6, 2008a.

harshly depicting the Khatami administration, he signaled that he was not in agreement with Iranian policies, including those on the nuclear issue, from 2003–2005—a striking admission, given his primacy in decisionmaking. In disowning that period and the search for common ground with the international community, he was clearly endorsing "resistance" and "steadfastness" and claiming responsibility for putting steel into the spines of his weak subordinates.[92] Khamenei has used the impact of the 2007 NIE, which had reduced (at least temporarily) the danger of severe consequences if Iran continues its current nuclear policy, to identify with Ahmadinejad's approach and to discredit the reformists and pragmatic conservatives.

Summary: Leadership Dynamics and Iranian Nuclear Policy

The nuclear question has revealed certain aspects of factionalism and personal interests in the Iranian decisionmaking system. There have been two very different views of what Iran's interests are, and there are two very different views of how the country should interact with the world: comply or confront. Although the reformists and the pragmatic conservatives do not necessarily view the nuclear program as being a zero-sum game, the principlists fear that compromise on the issue represents a generalized retreat in the face of Western pressure—a retreat that would entail a loss of legitimacy for the Islamic Republic.

In addition, nuclear policy has been tied to the fortunes of the principal faction that dominates Iranian politics. The salience of factional dynamics was clear in the case of Ahmadinejad. He exercised tight control over the nuclear issue by relegating key tactical decisions to a small circle of confidantes, and he used the confidantes' ties with the Supreme Leader to create and exploit a nuclear populism and to divert attention from Iran's economic woes. The nuclear issue has also been marked by personal rivalry. Larijani, having had his wings clipped by Ahmadinejad, tried to utilize his position as speaker of the Majles to reinsert himself into national-security policymaking.

---

[92] However, Ahmadinejad's victory in the 2005 election had little to do with foreign affairs.

Finally, the Supreme Leader has not remained above the fray on the nuclear issue: He prefers the principlists, perceiving them to be more loyal than the reformists or even the pragmatic conservatives, who are more likely to challenge his authority and post. He has taken a public stance on the nuclear issue, a stance that identifies him with what could be seen, due to continuing economic woes, as an administration that has failed on the domestic front.

Iran's foreign- and national-security policies appeared, until the 2009 election, to have enhanced the country's prestige abroad and burnished a domestic perception in Iran that the country is mounting steadfast resistance against bullying powers. However, despite having become less assailable in terms of his approach to foreign and security policies, Ahmadinejad and the government faced greater vulnerability over what some might characterize as mismanagement of Iran's economy. The Iranian economy has emerged as a primary factional battleground and will likely continue to remain so even after the 2009 presidential election, especially in light of the continuing global recession and Iran's diminished government revenues from petroleum exports. It is these bread-and-butter issues to which we now turn.

The Emergence of the Economy as a Factional Battleground

Iran's deteriorating economy has become the most contentious issue in Iranian domestic and factional politics. Ahmadinejad, who once promised to put oil money on the table of the average worker, has been blamed by many among Iran's elite for overseeing Iran's economic decline since his election.[93] Regardless of the outcome of confrontations over the results of the presidential election, the regime will continue to have many serious, systemic economic problems to address. The Iranian unemployment rate was estimated by the Iranian government to

---

[93] *Kayhan* (Tehran), unattributed report entitled "Ahmadinezhad in a Meeting with 140 Majlis Representatives: Oil Money Must Be Seen on the People's Table," June 21, 2005, in "Selection List—Persian Press Menu via Internet 21 Jun 05," Dialog/World News Connection 0209450646, June 21, 2005.

have reached 10.3 percent in 2007–2008, while some economists have estimated it to be as high as 25 percent in certain parts of the country.[94] At the same time, Iran has experienced an 80-percent jump over the past two decades in the number of young people entering the job market.[95] Official estimates of Iran's inflation rate have been as high as 27 percent,[96] and, according to one report, the price of real estate in Tehran has climbed by 200 percent since 2006.[97] International sanctions placed on Iran due to its continuation of uranium enrichment have further weakened the Iranian economy. Iranian businesspeople, for example, face great difficulties in obtaining letters of credit for international transactions, and they must rely on cash transactions to conduct everyday business.[98] The prevalence of inefficiency inherent in Iran's state-run economy, the corruption and lack of accountability, and a burgeoning black market make matters much worse for the average Iranian.

Ahmadinejad failed to deliver on his campaign promises to the very constituencies that he courted for support over the nuclear issue— the rural lower classes. The government's economic policies under Ahmadinejad arguably exacerbated the Islamic Republic's historically dysfunctional and often ailing economy. According to Ahmadinejad's former minister of finance, Davud Danesh-Jafari, the sudden and relatively massive infusion of oil cash into the economy in 2008 and the government's large expenditures on provincial infrastructure projects created the surging inflation rates currently bedeviling much of Iran's lower and middle classes. In addition, low interest rates under the Ahmadinejad administration encouraged banks to provide loans to many individuals and businesses without proper oversight, leading to "non-productive economic activities," such as overspeculation, in

---

[94] "Iran's Unemployment Falls to 10.3 pct—Minister," Reuters India, March 31, 2008.

[95] Crane et al., 2008, p. xvi.

[96] "Iran's Inflation Tops 27%," Agence France-Presse, September 7, 2008.

[97] Parisa Hafezi, "Latest Hot Housing Market: Tehran," *International Herald Tribune*, May 28, 2008.

[98] "Ayatollah Makarem Shirazi: Gerani Maskan Ghowgha Mikonad [Ayatollah Makarem Shirazi: The Housing Cost Has Raised an Uproar]," *Abrar* (Tehran), April 19, 2008.

real estate.[99] Finally, the administration's relative lack of technocratic and economic know-how—due largely to Ahmadinejad's penchant for placing loyalist ideologues in key government positions—made matters worse. Rather than integrating Iran's economy into the global market and, hence, obtaining desperately needed investments and expertise for Iran's energy sector, Ahmadinejad made the achievement of "social justice" his primary "economic" goal.

It may be unfair to entirely blame Iran's economic woes on Ahmadinejad alone. The Islamic Republic has never been known for efficient economic planning. The executive branch, headed by the president, has primary responsibility for economic planning, but the president's ability to craft and execute an economic plan is challenged by competing government institutions, such as the Majles, and by informal economic networks and parochial interests. In addition, the IRGC and the *bonyads*, which together account for a considerable portion of national economic activity, are largely beyond government oversight and control and are administered by networks and individuals whose economic interests may contradict the government's national economic goals. Even Danesh-Jafari, often critical of his former boss, Ahmadinejad, has noted the role of these interests in diminishing the Iranian government's economic performance.[100]

The Ahmadinejad administration and its supporters have employed arguments that reflect these endemic problems, especially widespread corruption, to deflect blame to both internal and external sources. These arguments have been infused with references to competing factions and personalities. In an April 2008 speech in Qom, Ahmadinejad spoke out against "economic mafias" and accused "a gentleman who still today has an important post at the center of power" of control-

---

[99] "Dar Marasem-e to'di': Che Bayad Kard? Jang-e Eghtesadi ra Doshman Aghaz Kardeh Boud [What Could Be Done? The Enemy Had Started Economic Warfare]," *Agahsazi News*, April 23, 2008.

[100]"Khorouj-e Akharin Vazir-e Tarafdar-e Eghtesad-e Azad az Kabineh [Exit of the Last Minister Supporting Free Market Economics from the Cabinet]," *Shahrvand-e Emrooz* (Tehran), April 20, 2008.

ling a nationwide cigarette smuggling network.[101] This was seen as an indirect attack on Rezai and, by inference, his close (and extremely wealthy) ally Rafsanjani. This was not a new tactic for Ahmadinejad: Over the years, he and his supporters have painted Iran's traditional elite as corrupt and largely responsible for Iran's chronic ills.

The pro-Ahmadinejad principlists' attempts to discredit the traditional conservative and pragmatic conservative elite culminated in an unprecedented public denunciation in June 2008 of senior Iranian figures by Abbas Palizdar, a presumed supporter of Ahmadinejad and member of the Majles Judicial Inquiry and Review Committee. Speaking at provincial universities in Hamedan and Shiraz, Palizdar revealed that conservative Iranian clergymen had used their connections to and influence in the Iranian government for personal profit. The accused clergymen included luminaries of the old men's club, including Ayatollah Mohammad Yazdi (former Chief of the Judiciary), Ayatollah Mohammad Emami Kashani (Tehran's provisional Friday-prayer leader), Hojjatoleslam Ali Akbar Natq Nouri (former Speaker of the Majles and Head of the Supreme Leader's Office for Investigations), and Rafsanjani.[102] Many of these individuals had publicly opposed Ahmadinejad's economic policies. Subsequently, Palizdar was attacked by the conservative media and arrested by the authorities for "spreading lies."[103] According to *Kayhan*, Palizdar was "part of a psychological warfare project planned by a so-called reformist group."[104]

The turmoil surrounding the Palizdar affair, which was remarkable for its public nature, is symptomatic of the deep-seated factional struggle taking place in Iran. The economic situation has led many of the Iranian elite—conservatives and reformists alike—to portray Ahmadinejad and his administration as grossly incompetent. Criticism of the government's economic performance has come not only from

---

[101] "He Meant Tomans, Not Dollars!" Roozonline.com, April 27, 2008.

[102] "The Accuser Is Accused, and Jailed," Iran Press Service, June 11, 2008. See also Thomas Erdbrink, "Iran Official Arrested for Criticizing Clerics," *The Washington Post*, June 12, 2008.

[103] "The Exposer Is Finally Arrested," Roozonline.com, June 13, 2008.

[104] "The Exposer Is Finally Arrested," 2008.

the usual Ahmadinejad opponents, such as Khatami and Rafsanjani, but also from traditional conservative figures, such as Mahdavi-Kani, and leading Qom clergymen, such as Ayatollahs Makarem-Shirazi and Mousavi Ardabili. Mahdavi-Kani, belittling Ahmadinejad's claim that the Hidden Imam was managing the government, stated that

> Mr. Ahmadinejad should not be saying such things because it creates a negative impression of Imam Mahdi in the eyes of the public. If it was Imam Mahdi who was running the show, then does this mean that he cannot get rid of the mafia? Is the 5,000 Toman price for rice also his doing? With all his greatness, Imam Khomeini never made such remarks about Imam Mahdi.[105]

After the president's "mafia" speech, Mahdavi-Kani warned Ahmadinejad against "misdirecting the blame" for high prices, and Danesh-Jafari denied the existence of a monopoly on cigarette imports and blamed Iran's economic woes on Ahmadinejad's policy of lowering interest rates.[106] Rezai struck back through his Tabnak Web site, which stated that "the history of such disclosures by the President indicates that he values propaganda and political results more than the truth."[107] Reformists alleged that Ahmadinejad was attempting to "deflect public criticism" in advance of the 2009 presidential election.[108]

Clearly, however, there are powerful, entrenched interests that benefit from the status quo—corruption, lack of accountability, and

---

[105]Arash Motamed, "Unsatisfactory Conditions and Imam Mahdi," Roozonline.com, May 19, 2008.

[106]Mohammad Reza Mahdavi-Kani, quoted in "Head of National Inspectorate Rejects President's Remarks on 'Economic Mafia,'" *Aftab-e Yazd* (Tehran) Web site, Dialog/World News Connection 0261251590, April 22, 2008a; Davoud Danesh-Jafari, quoted in Iranian Student's News Agency, April 24, 2008, in "Ahmadinezhad Speech Sparks Debate on Iran's Economic 'Mafia,'" Dialog/World News Connection 0262750025, May 22, 2008.

[107]Tabnak Web site, April 21, 2008, in "OSC Report: Ahmadinezhad Speech Sparks Debate on Iran's Economic 'Mafia,'" Dialog/World News Connection 0262750025, May 22, 2008.

[108]Ahmad Zeidabadi, Roozonline.com, April 23, 2008, in "Ahmadinezhad Speech Sparks Debate on Iran's Economic 'Mafia,'" Dialog/World News Connection 0262750025, May 22, 2008.

state control of the economy—and would likely present obstacles to any effort to reform the economy and put it on a better footing. Among these are the *bonyads*, the IRGC, those involved in corruption and the black market, and the state companies themselves. Influential personalities and power centers benefit from their ability to take in and disburse considerable amounts of oil money without government intervention, regardless of oil prices. Therefore, Ahmadinejad and his allies have been attacked not only by reformist and pragmatic conservative figures but also by traditional conservatives and principlists who initially had supported him; some of this criticism is genuine, but some is directed at Ahmadinejad's populist efforts to shake up the system. In fact, because of the entrenched interests, it is questionable whether any administration can make profound long-term changes and improvements to Iran's economy.

Summary: Leadership Dynamics and Iranian Economic Policy

Ahmadinejad's critics have accused him of failing to achieve the socio-economic promises of his 2005 presidential campaign. The factional maneuvering over the economy may have been intended to weaken Ahmadinejad ahead of the 2009 presidential election at a time when other policy areas—such as the Middle East and the nuclear issue—provide less-attractive fodder for the reformists and pragmatic conservatives, much less competitors among the principlists. However, Ahmadinejad has survived the political turmoil of the past four years and, in some ways, has emerged victorious. Come election time, he was able to claim that his policies had positioned Iran as a dominant regional power, notwithstanding the economic problems caused by the "economic mafias." In the end, however, Ahmadinejad's "reelection" was not determined by popular support for or dissatisfaction with him and his economic policies but rather by behind-the-scenes factional and power-center maneuvering (and, seemingly, fraud) meant to maintain the status quo and support Iran's ultimate decisionmaker, Supreme Leader Khamenei.

Concluding Remarks: Domestic Politics and Policymaking

The opaque nature of decisionmaking in Tehran, the parallel institutions, the bifurcation of the government between elected and appointed officials, the informal networks, the undercurrents of factional maneuvering—all lead the analyst to look for some key to unlock the secrets of regime policymaking. That such a key exists appears doubtful. Iran's political system and domestic politics will continue to be convoluted and often unpredictable. Institutional duplication, informal politics, factional disputes, and resulting stalemate preclude coherent, forward-looking policies. This creates a tendency toward inertia and an absence of initiative.

This chapter helps reveal or reinforce a number of observations about the relationship between policymaking and domestic politics. First, foreign policy and, more recently, economic policy are used to extend domestic power or weaken a rival. The main actors have distinctive policy orientations that reflect not only their inclinations and very profound and opposing visions of Iran's direction but also their narrower, personal interests. But these divisions themselves are not likely to produce major changes in Iran's overall foreign and security policies. Still, foreign policy is an essential component of the regime's identity and a source of its legitimacy; it takes second place to domestic bread-and-butter issues but is exploited in factional rivalries. Foreign-policy decisionmaking is largely an elite concern and activity.

Iran's factions have taken advantage of some issues, such as the nuclear program, for domestic purposes. By appealing to the public and raising the political stakes, Ahmadinejad has made nuclear and, increasingly, Middle East policies subject to popular approval. Once an issue is in the public domain, flexibility is lost. At the same time, the collective decisionmaking inherent in the deliberations of the SNSC becomes prevalent during times of crisis. This ensures that all factions and political decisionmakers take responsibility for unwise decisions.

The nature of consultation in Iranian decisionmaking is not a process that can be mapped in advance. Questions of whom to consult, when, and on what issues are decided in an ad hoc manner depending on the subject matter and the Supreme Leader's proclivities, preferences, and whims. New processes and routines may be established, as they were in nuclear case, during which the SNSC itself became the central coordinating agency. The only pattern is that there is no pattern.[109] As a result, the coalescence of major players on a given decision is virtually impossible to verify or predict, especially at a distance.

Finally, the Supreme Leader has the last word on security issues. The present principlist policies of nonengagement and defiance suit him ideologically, a tendency that presents a challenge to the Obama administration's efforts to open a dialogue with the regime. In openly siding with the radical Ahmadinejad faction that dominates the government, Khamenei may have ended the appearance of being a factional arbiter by identifying his position with that of the principlist tendency. A different Supreme Leader, working with a like-minded Iranian president, could shift Iran's foreign policies. However, this would entail taking on the constituencies and interest groups that benefit from the current status quo. For now, Iran's policy of defiance is perceived to have been successful and not in need of serious adjustment.

The 2009 election may preserve Iran's status as a "revolutionary" state for the time being. Pragmatic conservative and reformist figures who have called for more-moderate policies and the "rational" pursuit of national interests, such as Rafsanjani, Khatami, Mehdi Karrubi, and Mousavi, have been marginalized for the foreseeable future. Principlist power brokers from the Revolutionary Guards and Khamenei's inner circle will most likely play a dominant role in shaping Iran's foreign policies in the next few years.

---

[109] Former decisionmakers and insiders attest that they themselves do not know in advance who will be consulted or when (multiple author discussions with Iranian officials in Geneva, Paris, and London, 2002–2008).

CHAPTER SIX

Conclusion: Power and Politics in the Islamic Republic

In the preceding chapters, we explored the strategic culture of the elite in the Islamic Republic of Iran, described the formal institutions of government, examined the informal power centers and relationships that define Iranian policymaking, and assessed the role of factionalism in changes in key foreign- and domestic-policy arenas. In this concluding chapter, we summarize the most-important findings of our research.

Key Observations on How the Iranian Political System Works

The political system and decisionmaking processes of the Islamic Republic are commonly described as "opaque" by Western observers of Iran. These observers note that even Iranians themselves—particularly the *gheyr-e khodi*, the majority of the population—have difficulty making sense of how things get done in their government. Why is this? What makes Iranian decisionmaking and elite behavior more difficult to interpret and predict than those of, say, Pakistan, or Russia, or even the United States? In the following paragraphs, we offer some observations that might help provide insight into the answers to these questions, and we supply a different lens through which Western observers, analysts, and policymakers might view Iran.

The Informal Trumps the Formal and *Is* the System

When a student of the U.S. political system seeks to understand how that system works, he or she begins by examining the U.S. Constitution and analyzing the formal structures—the executive, legislative, and judicial branches—and the processes and relationships that bind those structures to create decisions, laws, and regulations that govern the country's domestic and foreign policies. Undoubtedly, there are informal relationships and levers of influence among U.S. policymakers that help determine the direction of these policies, but these other elements largely exist within and are limited by the formal rules of law and governance. So, the formal structure tends to drive analysis of U.S. (and Western) decisionmaking, and this allows for relatively straightforward categorization of decisionmaking processes based on the formal institutions that are responsible for and retain the authority to take decisions in specific areas of policy.

Not so with regard to Iran. Although the constitution of the Islamic Republic does set forth the roles and responsibilities of the various formal institutions of the government—and these bodies certainly have importance—the institutions serve primarily as a backdrop or playing field for informal give and take among the individuals, networks, and factions that the Supreme Leader oversees, brokers, and, at times, engages. Thus, the framework or lens through which outside analysts must view the Iranian system does not begin with the formal institutions but rather with the influence, experiences, and worldviews of and relationships among *khodi* individuals, their networks, and key power centers, such as the IRGC and the Haqqani clerical complex. These individuals and groups often use formal institutions to gain and maintain power, influence, and access to financial and other resources—all under the watchful eye of the Supreme Leader. This makes the examination of Iranian decisionmaking exceedingly difficult because back-channel maneuvering and bargaining are by nature hidden from view.

The Supreme Leader Retains the Most Power, but He Is Not Omnipotent

Western observers can fall prey to one of two misconceptions about the roles of the Supreme Leader and the president of Iran. The first is that the president has a great deal of power and retains a primary decisionmaking role on issues of both foreign and domestic policy. This misconception in part arises from a lack of understanding of the Iranian system and a tendency to mirror-image the U.S. system, but it is likely fueled by the fact that the president is most often the face of the government to the outside world. In recent times, Ahmadinejad has been both outspoken and outrageous in his speeches, his rambling letters to foreign heads of state, and his other public statements and activities. He is indeed trying to carve out greater power for his office (and for himself)—just as Khatami did before him with somewhat less success—but his statements should not automatically be accepted as official Iranian policy. The president is a participant in decisionmaking, but his level of independence depends to a great extent on the level of freedom the Supreme Leader chooses to grant him.

The second misconception is that the Supreme Leader is all-powerful—that he can dictate policies and make decisions based on his own preferences and that such policies and decisions will be implemented. Although it acknowledges that Khamenei is the most influential individual in Iran, this misconception misses the nuance with which Khamenei must wield his authority. Sadjadpour captures the Supreme Leader's role as follows:

> Neither a dictator nor a democrat—but with traits of both— Khamenei is the single most powerful individual in a highly factionalized, autocratic regime. Though he does not make national decisions on his own, neither can any major decisions be taken without his consent.[1]

Khatami's failure as president to open civil society and to pursue relations with the West was a clear example of Khamenei's power to prevent Iranian domestic and foreign policy from changing in ways that contradicted his own worldview.

Khamenei's power derives from a number of sources, including his own broad networks of representatives, appointees, and confidantes;

---

[1]   Sadjadpour, 2008, p. 1.

his role as commander-in-chief; and his very position as Supreme Leader. But, lacking the iconic status and charisma of Khomeini, he must balance a multitude of competing interests to ensure that no single faction or group becomes so dominant that it threatens his power and prerogatives. For example, while Khamenei has tended to favor an executive branch dominated by principlists under Ahmadinejad, he has also made sure to balance their power by enhancing the role of the Expediency Council under Rafsanjani—a role, however, that will likely diminish with Rafsanjani's recently weakened influence. Thus, to ensure his own power and centrality, Khamenei maintains what is a relatively dysfunctional political system that tends toward stasis, where the absence of forward movement and innovation in the system is normal—or maybe even desired. Balance among interest groups is the guarantor of the Supreme Leader's indispensability.

Factional Competition Drives Political Discourse and Policymaking

The Supreme Leader therefore encourages factional rivalry as long as it does not threaten the system. The factions, in turn, operate within the limits needed to preserve the Islamic regime, but survival of the regime is the point at which the so-called consensus ends. Factional maneuvering is a key manifestation of the competition for power and influence, and foreign- and domestic-policy issues are used as tools and are extensions of this competition. The 2009 election dispute showed, however, that factional disputes can destabilize the system and that consensus on regime survival may not be enough to prevent elite conflicts in the future.

Factions use foreign policy to promote their domestic agendas. For example, Khatami and the reformists pursued normalization and a dialogue of civilizations to open up Iranian society, and Ahmadinejad and the principlists have pursued confrontation and increased political repression. At the same time, the Ahmadinejad administration has downplayed the idea that the United States might attack Iran over its nuclear program because of the U.S. "quagmire" in Iraq, the 2007 NIE, and the wide range of military means that Iran can use to defend itself and to hit back. This apparent contradiction has left the principlists wide open to attack on the economy, an opening the reformists and pragmatic conservatives have sought to exploit.

But factional differences over foreign and domestic policies are, at their core, an ongoing battle between fundamental differences over what Iran should become. This battle engenders a debate about the essence of the state and the legitimacy and staying power of the Islamic Revolution. Contention between the two visions—one emphasizing the Islamic *Revolution* and a model of resistance and self-sufficiency, the other emphasizing the Islamic *Republic* and a model of a normal state seeking independent development—will endure for years to come. At the time of writing (soon after the June 2009 presidential election), the revolutionary mind-set in Iranian politics was clearly ascendant.

We have also noted that factions are not "teams" with the same line-up on every issue. Factions in Iran are really supernetworks composed of individuals, informal networks, and power centers that coalesce around specific issues based on worldview and self-interest. These individuals and networks adapt to changing circumstances and at times may change colors if doing so will improve their position and influence in the system. Thus, it is difficult, though not impossible, to determine in advance how alliances will form around specific issues.

The Iranian system is brutally competitive. The overlapping formal authorities and informal decisionmaking processes make for a relatively stable regime, but the prevalence of factional competition also results in strategic incoherence, mixed signals, and even contradictory public statements. Domestic politics are of primary concern to the elites, and the elites invest a great deal of energy in internal competition rather than in setting a coherent policy agenda.

Iran's Domestic Power Politics Are Highly Dynamic and Periodic

In each of the three decades since the revolution, a different power center has gained greater influence in relation to others, and this influence has ebbed and flowed. During the Khomeini era and the Iran-Iraq War, the clerics appeared to enjoy a period of primacy. The 1990s were the era of the *bonyads*, especially in terms of economic influence, with the clerics still continuing to wield considerable political influence. The Revolutionary Guards appear to have dominated during the first decade of the millennium, using Iran's increased emphasis on security issues as a political and economic lever. A new generation of lay leaders with an IRGC pedigree—Ahmadinejad, Larijani, Qalibaf, and others—has arisen to pose a challenge to clerics and to the old guard. In the 1980s and 1990s, the most-valuable connections were ties to the clerics, but now they are ties to the Guards. The IRGC and the Basij increasingly insert themselves into politics and business. However, as with any power center in Iran, the IRGC is not monolithic. Senior commanders appointed by the Supreme Leader might be revolutionary "fire-breathers," but others among the rank-and-file may be more representative of the larger society of Iran, with many (including those who fought in the Iran-Iraq War) espousing a more pragmatic view of the world.

As the present decade draws to a close, it is natural to ask, "What comes next?" Will the pattern repeat itself a fourth time, with some other power center eclipsing the IRGC, or will the IRGC continue to dominate and thereby break the pattern of the previous three decades? We turn to these questions below in our discussion of key trends emerging in the Islamic Republic.

Emerging Trends to Watch in Iran

Our research identified three trends that appear to be emerging as key determinants of the future direction of the Islamic Republic of Iran. We pose these trends as questions because either they have not played out or their implications have yet to become clear. We also present some conjectures that might help frame U.S. thinking about formulating future policy vis-à-vis the Islamic Republic, although we note that such guesswork on the subject of Iran can only be very tentative.

The Revolutionary Guards: Will They Rise or Fall?

As the third decade of the Islamic Revolution comes to a close, the future role of the IRGC arises as a key question. The IRGC has become a domestic political, economic, and security power, and members and alumni have pervaded the government and other sectors of society. In Chapter Four, we describe the emergence of a spectrum of mind-sets about the environment in which the IRGC operates. One view is more security-conscious, with holders of this mind-set seeing the existence of a geostrategic battle between Iran and the United States for power and influence in the region and wanting to pursue confrontation to secure the "rights" of Iran and the survival of the Islamic Revolution. Others in the IRGC are more profit-oriented and are focused on securing lucrative business ventures. Although they agree that Iran is engaged in a strategic competition with the United States, they believe that the rivalry between the two countries can be eased in the name of a more positive commercial environment.

What future might evolve from this situation? In the view of the Guards, is there a modus vivendi with Khamenei but not necessarily with a new Supreme Leader? If the Guards continue to gain political power, they could begin to see themselves as kingmakers and demand more from the Supreme Leader and the clerics. Or, the IRGC may—especially if it is at the apex of its domestic influence when Khamenei dies—make a bid for power in the next several years, possibly even challenging the Assembly of Experts in selecting the next Supreme Leader. The second scenario could be quite worrisome if the Islamic Republic were to attain the capacity to build and deploy nuclear weapons. An energized, adventurous, nuclear-armed IRGC that is dominant in Iranian domestic and foreign policymaking but whose commander in chief is a weak Supreme Leader may pose a more pointed threat to U.S. interests in the region. The aftermath of the 2009 election may propel Iran toward a more-militarized future, with the Revolutionary Guards playing a dominant role in the Iranian political system.

Alternatively, an increase in the IRGC's focus on economic power could lead it to become an institution that is greedy and bloated, less flexible, and more risk averse. Such an emphasis on business could cause the Guards to see greater utility in regional stability and reduced tensions with the United States and the West. It could also increase the likelihood that the IRGC would be eclipsed by a fourth power center. One candidate for such a dominant group could be a new alliance of technocrats—some of whom, like Larijani and Qalibaf, have ties to both the IRGC and other power centers—who emphasize good management of government and the economy but retain appropriate ideological and political credentials so as to separate themselves from Ahmadinejad and Rafsanjani.[2]

The Old Guard: Vulnerable to Challenge?

A second trend to watch over the next few years is the evolution of the relationship between the older generation of the men's club, which helped Khomeini overthrow the Shah and establish the Islamic Republic, and a younger cohort of lay leaders (with some clerical allies) who were shaped primarily by the Iran-Iraq War and are less beholden to the establishment. The leaders of the older generation are entrenched politically and financially and do not retire voluntarily from politics. Yet, as gatekeepers, they are also instrumental in admitting the newer generation to the club. Now, the new leaders are seeking to carve out their own centers of influence, sometimes in ways that may challenge the positions and power of their elders. Ahmadinejad's populist outreach to heretofore untapped rural classes in the provinces and his complaints about "economic mafias" can be partially understood in this context. Of course, at some point in the future, this older generation will pass naturally from the scene. The question is whether its members will be forced out before that time and, if so, what this might mean for the Iranian system.

Clearly, the men's club has survived for three decades because of its cohesion when threatened and its members' penchant for adapting as a group and as individuals. Rafsanjani is an example of how adaptable this group of leaders tends to be: Unable even to win one of 30 seats from Tehran in the 2000 Majles elections, he almost won the presidency in 2005 and gained leadership of the Assembly of Experts and the Expediency Council. Other individuals have broadened their ties to and support of multiple, even competing, groups. Khamenei has built ties to people, such as Ahmadinejad, who have challenged the establishment in which the Supreme Leader himself is so invested. Several interpretations of this move are possible, but a notable one is that the Supreme Leader has sought to control the new generation in an

---

[2]   Author telephone discussion with an Iran scholar, March 4, 2008.

attempt to bring it into the fold slowly without threatening the status quo and his own position.

The Next Supreme Leader: Who or What Will Succeed Khamenei?

By 2009, Khamenei will have held the position of Supreme Leader for two-thirds of the Islamic Republic's existence. He will have presided over three very different presidential administrations and have guided the country through seven years of momentous change in its neighborhood and through international condemnation and isolation over its nuclear program. He is an extremely experienced Supreme Leader. But he turns 70 years old in 2009, and rumors about his deteriorating health have recently surfaced. The nature of the succession when he passes from the scene will be difficult to predict. Will the transition be smooth, or will it be marked by conflict that destabilizes the system? What kind of successor will be selected—a "compromise candidate," like Khamenei, who will not rock the boat? How might the office of Supreme Leader evolve?

The next Supreme Leader will be a primary determinant of how the other two trends evolve. The scope of his power and the level of his influence within the system will be critical factors in determining Iran's future direction, particularly with regard to relations with the United States and with other states in the region. A relatively strong leader may continue the status quo or steer the country toward gradual change (for ill or good, depending on one's perspective), whereas a weak leader could be exploited or dominated by other power centers, such as the IRGC. In the latter case, the very nature of the Islamic Republic could change drastically and in potentially destabilizing ways. This is especially worrisome given the increasing militarization of Iranian politics. In our view, therefore, the internal discussions and activities surrounding the succession of the Supreme Leader constitute the most important development for U.S. and Western policymakers and analysts to watch as a harbinger of the future direction of the Islamic Republic.

Concluding Thoughts for U.S. Policymakers

The United States—its presence and intentions in the region, its status in the world—is the key antagonist and source of policy debate and formulation in the Islamic Republic. One could even submit that the Iranian elite are obsessed with U.S. statements, actions, and reactions and that perceptions of potential U.S. responses drive the major foreign-policy, and, at times, domestic-policy, decisions. In fact, Washington's responses to statements or posturing from Tehran can enhance the importance of an issue within Iran beyond its inherent relevance, and factions use this phenomenon to their own advantage. External developments greatly affect Iranian domestic politics because Iranian politicians and factions speak to constituents and address each other through foreign- and domestic-policy debates as they jockey for advantage within the elite.

It is therefore incumbent on U.S. policymakers to couch their communications with and about Iran in ways that are nuanced and that consider how their statements might be perceived in Tehran (and by whom). The United States is at a distinct disadvantage because its diplomats and citizens lack broad access to the Islamic Republic and, thus, to intimate knowledge of its inner workings. For this reason, it is imperative that U.S. policymakers avoid trying to play or leverage the domestic politics of Iran and that they deal with the government of the day, not with the people or power centers Washington would prefer. The ability of the United States to correctly determine the effects of its purposeful efforts to shore up the moderates in Iran is extremely limited, and the strategy could backfire if it undermines the very people it seeks to support. An example of a cautious approach was Obama's initial hesitation to harshly criticize the government's crackdown on protesters. Such criticism could have been classified as U.S. "interference" and used against reformists by the hard-liners.

If Iranian relations with the United States and the international community become more normalized in the future, U.S. policymakers must take as an article of faith that dealing with Iran does not necessarily mean dealing with a unitary actor. Normal relations with the United States would be a radical departure for Iran's elites, and they would need to recognize and accept these relations as necessary both for Iran (and for the survival of the Islamic Revolution) *and* their own power and influence (and that of the patronage networks upon which they rely). Factional politics make openings for dialogue and a stable U.S.-Iranian relationship difficult. Increased engagement with the United States and the West would have domestic consequences for Iran and create winners and losers, and the latter would not necessarily acquiesce willingly, even if the Supreme Leader fully supported such engagement. There are entrenched political, economic, social, and religious interests that see great merit in the status quo and great threat in opening Iran to the United States. Therefore, the United States should expect that powerful interest groups in Iran will attempt to torpedo efforts toward a rapprochement between the two countries, and it should plan accordingly. The extent to which the United States and Iran would need to worry about attempts by domestic Iranian groups to derail emerging U.S.-Iranian relations would depend on the breadth of the consensus for engagement across Iranian factions.

Competing government structures and power centers in Iran would make U.S. negotiations with the Islamic Republic exceedingly difficult. Iranian negotiators may or may not have the authority to reach agreements, and ensuring that Washington is dealing with the "right" representatives of the Iranian regime would be a critical task for U.S. negotiating teams. Iranian negotiators may be looking over their shoulders at decisionmakers in Tehran, as was the case during nuclear negotiations in the waning months of the Khatami administration. Or, these negotiators may reflect contradictions and indecision within the Iranian regime, as Larijani's tenure as chief nuclear negotiator demonstrated. However, these difficulties do not mean that such negotiations on nuclear or other issues are not worthwhile. As Iran scholar John Limbert contends, "Talking, hard and disagreeable as it might be, is likely to be more productive than continuing 28 years of noisy and sometimes violent confrontation."[3] One key for the United States

---

[3] John W. Limbert, "Negotiating with the Islamic Republic of Iran: Raising the Chances for Success—Fifteen Points to Remember," United States Institute of Peace, Special Report No. 199, January 2008, p. 4.

is to enter such discussions armed with a nuanced view of the complex system of government and politics that the Iranian interlocutors across the negotiating table represent.

Bibliography

Adib-Moghaddam, Arshin, "Islamic Utopian Romanticism and the Foreign Policy Culture of Iran," *Critique: Critical Middle East Studies*, Vol. 14, No. 3, Fall 2005.

Afriasabi, Kavey, and Kayhan Bozorgmehr, "The View from Iran," *The Boston Globe*, December 5, 2007.

Aftab-e Yazd (Tehran) Web site, January 25, 2007, in "Critics Berate Ahmadinezhad for Complacency over Threats to Iran," Dialog/World News Connection 0238750465, January 27, 2007a.

———, October 21, 2007, in BBC Monitoring, October 24, 2007b.

———, November 29, 2007, in BBC Monitoring, December 3, 2007c.

Aftabnews (Tehran) Web site, April 4, 2007, in "OSC Analysis: Iran—Domestic Media Praise, Criticize Government's Handling of Crisis with Britain," Dialog/World News Connection 0242201037, April 6, 2007a.

———, April 6, 2007, in "OSC Analysis: Iran: Hardliners Play Down Opponents' Warnings of U.S. Military Strike," Dialog/World News Connection 0242801514, April 18, 2007b.

Aga'i, Sasan, "Why Larijani Left," *E'temad-e Melli* (Tehran), October 24, 2007, in BBC Monitoring, October 26, 2007.

"Ahmadinejad: 'Iran Ready to Fill Iraq Power Vacuum,'" *The Guardian* (London), August 28, 2007.

Ahmadinejad, Mahmoud, Vision of the Islamic Republic of Iran News Network 2, January 2, 2007, in BBC Monitoring, January 3, 2007a.

———, interview with Vision of the Islamic Republic of Iran Network 2, January 23, 2007, in "Critics Berate Ahmadinezhad for Complacency over Threats to Iran," Dialog/World News Connection 0238750465, January 27, 2007b.

———, "Speech to Supreme Leader," Vision of the Islamic Republic of Iran Network 1, July 2, 2007, in BBC Monitoring, July 3, 2007c.

————, "Address to the UN," Islamic Republic News Agency, September 26, 2007d.

————, Mehr News Agency, December 5, 2007, in BBC Monitoring, December 6, 2007e.

————, Islamic Republic News Agency Web site, February 11, 2008, in BBC Monitoring, February 12, 2008a.

————, Vision of the Islamic Republic of Iran Network 1, February 11, 2008, in BBC Monitoring, February 13, 2008b.

————, quoted on the Hemayat Web site, March 10, 2008, in "Iran Commentary Speaks on Different Approaches to Revolution," BBC Monitoring, March 11, 2008c.

————, "Resistance as the Only Way to Defeat the Zionists," Islamic Republic News Agency Web site, March 10, 2008, in BBC Monitoring, March 11, 2008d.

"Ahmadinezhad Vows Iran Will 'Smash the Face of Any Tyrant,'" Vision of the Islamic Republic of Iran Khuzestan Provincial TV, January 2, 2007, in BBC Monitoring, January 3, 2007.

Akhavi, Shahrough, *Religion and Politics in Contemporary Iran: Clergy-State Relations in the Pahlavi Period*, Albany, N.Y.: State University of New York Press, 1980.

al-Hoseyni, Seyyed Hasan, "The Global Mission and a Few Points," *E'temad-e Melli* (Tehran), April 15, 2008, in "Iran Paper Criticizes Ahmadinezhad's Efforts to Change 'World Management,'" BBC Monitoring, April 19, 2008.

al-Rashid, Abd al-Rahman, "Comments on Iranian Policy Under Khatami," *al-Sharq al-Awsat* (London) Web site, January 7, 2008, in BBC Monitoring, January 8, 2008.

al-Thaydi, Mshari, "Uhadhir an Taqdhi Alihi al-Ama'im [Warning Against the Religious Establishment]," *al-Sharq al-Awsat* (London), July 19, 2007.

Amirahmadi, Hooshang, "From Political Islam to National Secularism," Abadan Publishing Co., January 11, 2006.

Amirpur, Katajun, "The Future of Iran's Reform Movement," in Walter Posch, ed., *Iranian Challenges*, European Union Institute for Security Studies, Chaillot Paper No. 89, May 2006.

Amuzegar, Jahangir, "The Ahmadinejad Era: Preparing for the Apocalypse," *Journal of International Affairs*, Vol. 60, No. 2, Spring/Summer 2007.

Anonymous member of the "Independent Principle-ists' Current," quoted in *Farhang-e Ashti* (Tehran), February 7, 2008, in "OSC Analysis: Iran—Rifts Among Conservatives Intensify as Elections Approach," Dialog/World News Connection 0258501457, February 26, 2008.

"Ansar-e Hizballah," Radio Free Europe/Radio Liberty, December 7, 2004.

Ansari, Ali M., "Iran and the U.S. in the Shadow of 9/11: Persia and the Persian Question Revisited," *Iranian Studies*, Vol. 39, No. 2, June 2006.

—————, *Iran Under Ahmadinejad: The Politics of Confrontation*, International Institute for Strategic Studies, *Adelphi Paper* No. 393, 2007.

"Ansar-i Hizbullah: Followers of the Party of God," Globalsecurity.org, undated. As of February 4, 2008:
http://www.globalsecurity.org/intell/world/iran/ansar.htm

"A Rival for Iran's Ahmadinejad," *Time Magazine*, March 18, 2008.

"A Step Towards Convergence," Resalat Web site, February 21, 2008, in "Iran Paper Praises Government for Re-Establishing Ties with Arabs," BBC Monitoring, February 25, 2008.

"Ayatollah Makarem Shirazi: Gerani Maskan Ghowgha Mikonad [Ayatollah Makarem Shirazi: The Housing Cost Has Raised an Uproar]," *Abrar* (Tehran), April 19, 2008.

Azimi, Negar, "Hard Realities of Soft Power," *Iran Emrooz* (Tehran), June 24, 2007.

"Basij to Help Police Enhance Security in Iran," Fars News Agency, Dialog/World News Connection 0262800517, May 23, 2008.

Baztab, January 24, 2007, in "OSC Analysis: Critics Berate Ahmadinezhad for Complacency over Threats to Iran," Dialog/World News Connection 0238750465, January 27, 2007.

BBC News, "Iran: Who Holds the Power?" Web page, undated. As of September 9, 2008:
http://news.bbc.co.uk/2/shared/spl/hi/middle_east/03/iran_power/html/supreme_leader.stm

Begli Beigie, A. R., "Repeating Mistakes: Britain, Iran & the 1919 Treaty," *The Iranian*, March 27, 2001.

Benab, Younes Parsa, "The Origin and Development of Imperialist Contention in Iran; 1884–1921," Iran Chamber Society, June 11, 2008.

Bill, James A., *The Politics of Iran: Groups, Classes and Modernization*, Columbus, Ohio: Charles E. Merrill Publishing Company, 1972.

Bozorgmehr, Najmeh, "Khamene'i Urged to Rein in President," *Financial Times* (London), November 13, 2007.

—————, "President Hostage to His Promises," *Financial Times* (London), February 28, 2008a.

————, "Ayatollah Ensures Results Confirm His Absolute Supremacy," *Financial Times* (London), March 19, 2008b.

Bozorgmehr, Najmeh, and Roula Khalaf, "Dismay as Top Nuclear Official Quits," *Financial Times* (London), October 22, 2007a.

————, "Supreme Leader Keeps Watchful Eye as Ahmadinejad Consolidates Power," *Financial Times* (London), October 25, 2007b.

————, "Sanctions Net Still Hanging over Iran," *Financial Times* (London), December 5, 2007c.

Bronner, Ethan, "Hamas Is Undertaking Broad Military Buildup; Iran and Syria Helping, Israeli Study Finds," *International Herald Tribune*, April 10, 2008.

Buchta, Wilfried, *Who Rules Iran? The Structure of Power in the Islamic Republic*, Washington, D.C.: The Washington Institute for Near East Policy and the Konrad Adenauer Stiftung, 2000.

————, *Iran's Security Sector: An Overview*, Geneva Center for the Democratic Control of Armed Forces, Working Paper No. 146, August 2004.

Bureau of International Affairs, "Acquaintance with the Head of the Judiciary and His Viewpoints," Web page, undated. As of November 16, 2009: http://www.bia-judiciary.ir/bia-en/tabid/209/Default.aspx

Byman, Daniel, Shahram Chubin, Anoushiravan Ehteshami, and Jerrold D. Green, *Iran's Security Policy in the Post-Revolutionary Era*, Santa Monica, Calif.: RAND Corporation, MR-1320-OSD, 2001. As of July 20, 2009: http://www.rand.org/pubs/monograph_reports/MR1320/

Central Intelligence Agency, *The World Factbook: Iran*, 2008. As of May 22, 2008: https://www.cia.gov/library/publications/the-world-factbook/geos/ir.html#People

Chubin, Shahram, *Iran's Nuclear Ambitions*, Washington, D.C.: Carnegie Endowment for International Peace, 2006.

————, "Iran: Domestic Politics and Nuclear Choices," in Tellis and Wills, 2007.

————, *Iran's "Risktaking" in Perspective*, Institut Français des Relations Internationales, Proliferation Paper No. 21, Winter 2008.

Coalition Provisional Authority, *English Translation of Terrorist Musab al Zarqawi Letter Obtained by United States Government in Iraq*, February 2004.

Collier, Robert, "Nuclear Weapons Unholy, Iran Says," *San Francisco Chronicle*, October 31, 2003.

Colvin, Marie, "Hamas Wages Iran's Proxy War on Israel: A Hamas Leader Admits Hundreds of His Fighters Have Travelled to Tehran," *Sunday Times* (London), March 9, 2008.

Cordesman, Anthony H., *Iran's Developing Military Capabilities*, Washington D.C.: The Center for Strategic and International Studies, 2005.

Cordesman, Anthony H., and Martin Kleiber, *Iran's Military Forces and Warfighting Capabilities: The Threat in the Northern Gulf*, Washington, D.C.: Center for Strategic and International Studies, 2007.

Crane, Keith, Rollie Lal, and Jeffrey Martini, *Iran's Political, Demographic, and Economic Vulnerabilities*, Santa Monica, Calif.: RAND Corporation, MG-693-AF, 2008. As of July 31, 2009:
http://www.rand.org/pubs/monographs/MG693/

Danesh-Jafari, Davoud, quoted in Iranian Student's News Agency, April 24, 2008, in "Ahmadinezhad Speech Sparks Debate on Iran's Economic 'Mafia,'" Dialog/World News Connection 0262750025, May 22, 2008.

"Dar Marasem-e to'di': Che Bayad Kard? Jang-e Eghtesadi ra Doshman Aghaz Kardeh Boud [What Could Be Done? The Enemy Had Started Economic Warfare]," Agahsazi News, April 23, 2008.

Daragahi, Borzou, "Iran's Inner and Outer Circles of Influence and Power," *The Los Angeles Times*, December 31, 2007.

Dareini, Ali Akbar, "Rafsanjani to Head Iranian Clerical Body," Associated Press, September 4, 2007.

———, "Iran's Ex-Nuke Negotiator Slams Ahmadinejad's Nuclear, Foreign Strategy," Associated Press, February 27, 2008.

Debate on al-Jazeera TV, January 19, 2008, in BBC Monitoring, January 25, 2008.

Djalili, Mohammad-Reza, "L'Iran d'Ahmadinejad: Évolutions Interne et Politique Étrangère [Ahmadinejad's Iran: Internal Developments and Foreign Policy]," *Politique Étrangère*, Spring 2007.

Dobbins, James, "Negotiating with Iran," in Green, Wehrey, and Wolf, 2009.

Dombey, Daniel, and Harvey Morris, "U.S. Sees Tehran Nuclear Dispute Going into 2009," *Financial Times* (London), February 27, 2008.

Eddie, Nikki, *Modern Iran: Roots and Results of a Revolution*, New Haven, Conn.: Yale University Press, 2006.

Ehteshami, Anoush, and Mahjoob Zweiri, eds., *Iran's Foreign Policy: From Khatami to Ahmadinejad*, Ithaca, N.Y.: Ithaca Press, 2008.

Eisenstadt, Michael, "The Armed Forces of the Islamic Republic of Iran," *Middle East Review of International Affairs*, Vol. 5, No. 1, March 2001.

El-Khodary, Taghreed, and Isabel Kershner, "As Israeli Forces Withdraw from Northern Gaza, Hamas Celebrates Its Rocketry," *The New York Times*, March 4, 2008.

Encyclopædia Britannica Online, "Treaty of Golestān," *Encyclopædia Britannica*, no date available. As of October 7, 2008:
http://www.britannica.com/EBchecked/topic/249210/Treaty-of-Golestan

Erdbrink, Thomas, "Iran Official Arrested for Criticizing Clerics," *The Washington Post*, June 12, 2008.

Esfandiari, Golnaz, "Iran: Warnings Hint at Greater Role by Revolutionary Guard in Muzzling Critics," Radio Free Europe/Radio Liberty, October 5, 2007.

———, "Iran: Political Activists to Steer Clear of Possible U.S. Funding," Radio Free Europe/Radio Liberty, April 4, 2008.

———, "Rafsanjani Turns to Iran's Supreme Leader to Deal With Ahmadinejad's 'Lies,'" Radio Free Europe/Radio Liberty, June 10, 2009. As of September 30 2009:
http://www.rferl.org/content/Former_Iranian_President_Turns_To_Supreme_Leader_To_Deal_With_Ahmadinejads_Lies/1751216.html

E'temad-e Melli (Tehran), December 10, 2007, in BBC Monitoring, December 12, 2007.

———, February 12, 2008, in BBC Monitoring, February 15, 2008.

Farhang-e Ashti (Tehran), November 22, 2007, in BBC Monitoring, November 28, 2007.

Fathi, Nazila, "Critique of Iranian Leader Reveals Political Rift," *The New York Times*, November 23, 2007a.

———, "Former Iranian President Publicly Assails Ahmadinejad," *The New York Times*, December 12, 2007b.

Fathi, Nazila, and Bowley, Graham, "New Post for Rival of President of Iran," *The New York Times*, May 29, 2008.

Fathi, Nazila, and Michael Slackman, "Iran's Nuclear Envoy Resigns: Talks in Doubt," *International Herald Tribune*, October 22, 2007.

Friday Sermon, Voice of the Islamic Republic of Iran, March 14, 2008, in BBC Monitoring, March 17, 2008.

Gable, Richard W., "Culture and Administration in Iran," *Middle East Journal*, Vol. 13, No. 4, Fall 1959.

Ghafarizadeh, Ezatollah, "Comments on Iran as a Model for Hezbollah," *Kayhan* (Tehran) Web site, April 23, 2008, in BBC Monitoring, April 28, 2008.

Ghaffari, Hanif, "The Biased Criticism on Foreign Policy," *Resalat* Web site, February 20, 2008, in "Iran Columnist Analyzes Foreign Policy Criticisms by Former Official," BBC Monitoring, February 22, 2008a.

————, *Resalat* Web site, February 20, 2008, in BBC Monitoring, February 25, 2008b.

Gheytanchi, Elham, and Babak Rahimi, "Iran's Reformists and Activists: Internet Exploiters," *Middle East Policy*, Vol. 15, No. 1, Spring 2008.

GlobalSecurity.org, "Shias in Iraq," Web page, last updated on June 22, 2005. As of June 12, 2008:
http://www.globalsecurity.org/military/world/iraq/religion-shia1.htm

Goodman, Adam, "Iran: Informal Networks and Leadership Politics," Advanced Research and Assessment Group, Defence Academy of the United Kingdom, Middle East Series No. 08/12, April 2008.

Green, Jerrold D., Frederic Wehrey, and Charles Wolf, Jr., *Understanding Iran*, Santa Monica, Calif.: RAND Corporation, MG-771-SRF, 2009. As of August 4, 2009:
http://www.rand.org/pubs/monographs/MG771/

Hafezi, Parisa, "Iran Hardliners Criticize Khatami's 'Insulting' Speech," Reuters, May 7, 2008a.

————, "Latest Hot Housing Market: Tehran," *International Herald Tribune*, May 28, 2008b.

Halliday, Fred, "Arabian Peninsula Opposition Movements," Middle East Research and Information Project, February 1985.

————, "Arabs and Persians Beyond the Geopolitics of the Gulf," *Cahiers d'Études sur la Méditerranée Orientale et le Mond Turco-Iranien*, March 4, 2005.

Hashim, Wahid, comments at "Iran on the Horizon, Panel II: Iran and the Gulf," Middle East Institute Conference Series, Middle East Institute, Washington, D.C., February 1, 2008.

"He Meant Tomans, Not Dollars!" Roozonline.com, April 27, 2008. As of August 12, 2008:
http://www.roozonline.com/english/news/newsitem/article/2008/april/27//he-meant-tomans-not-dollars.html

Hezbollah News Web site, February 3, 2008, in BBC Monitoring, February 5, 2008.

Hoseyni, Mohammad Ali, quoted in Fars News Agency, June 1, 2008, in "OSC Report: Iran—Critics Use IAEA Report to Suggest Larger Role for Majles," Dialog/World News Connection 263451475, June 5, 2008.

Hughes, Robin, "Iran Replenishes Hizbullah's Arms Inventory," *Jane's Defence Weekly*, January 3, 2007a.

————, "Tehran Fires Tor-M1," *Jane's Defense Weekly*, February 14, 2007b.

International Crisis Group, "Iran: The Struggle for the Revolution's Soul," *Middle East Report*, No. 5, August 2002.

————, "Iran: Ahmadinejad's Tumultuous Presidency," *Middle East Briefing*, No. 21, February 6, 2007.

"International: Hard Centres, Iranian Conservatives," *Economist*, Vol. 365, No. 8304, December 21, 2002.

"Iran Accuses U.S. of Supporting Rebel Groups," Agence France-Presse, September 6, 2007.

Iran Chamber Society, "Reza Shah Pahlavi," Web page, undated. As of June 11, 2008:
http://www.iranchamber.com/history/reza_shah/reza_shah.php

"Iran: Conservatives Claim Victory, but President Faces New Challenges," Radio Free Europe/Radio Liberty, March 17, 2008.

"Iran Deplores UAE Claim on 3 Islands," Islamic Republic News Agency, April 17, 2008.

"Iran President Attends Army Day, Pays Tribute to the Armed Forces," Vision of the Islamic Republic of Iran Network 1, April 17, 2008, in BBC Monitoring, April 17, 2008.

"Iran Press: Ex-Nuclear Chief Criticizes 'Ideological' Impact on Foreign Policy," Baztab News & Information Center Web site quoted on *E'temad-e Melli* (Tehran) Web site, July 23, 2006, in BBC Monitoring, July 24, 2006.

"Iran Report," Radio Free Europe/Radio Liberty, August 8, 2005.

"Iran: Senior Cleric Favours 'National Conciliation' After Post-Election Unrest," Iran Online, Dialog/World News Connection 0283200022, July 5, 2009.

"Iran Stakes Claim to Bahrain: Public Seeks 'Reunification . . . with Its Motherland,'" WorldTribune.com, July 13, 2007.

"Iran: They Think They Have Right on Their Side," *Economist*, November 24, 2007.

Iran TV Channel 1, February 23, 2008, in BBC Monitoring, February 25, 2008.

"Iran Welcomes Bonn Agreement on Afghanistan Despite Its 'Weak Points,'" Islamic Republic News Agency, December 7, 2001.

"Iranian Army to Help Build Metro in Northwestern Province," Vision of the Islamic Republic of Iran East Azarbayjan Provincial TV, Dialog/World News Connection 0271550922, November 14, 2008.

"Iranian Former Guards' Commander Says U.S. Greed Only Problem of Region," Vision of the Islamic Republic of Iran Network 1, February 12, 2008, in BBC Monitoring February 12, 2008.

"Iranian Intelligence Ministry Closely Monitoring Foreigners' Subversive Activities: Minister," Mehr News Agency, July 3, 2007.

"Iranian MPs Reject Oil Minister," BBC News, November 23, 2005.

Iranian Student's News Agency Web site, December 10, 2007, in BBC Monitoring, December 13, 2007a.

————, December 12, 2007, in BBC Monitoring, December 14, 2007b.

"Iranian Transportation Ministry Denies Blaming IRGC for Closure of New Airport," Islamic Republic News Agency Web site, Dialog/World News Connection 0194750650, August 31, 2004.

"Iran's Aggressive Foreign Policy Based on Wisdom," Islamic Republic News Agency Web site, December 10, 2007, in BBC Monitoring, December 10, 2007.

"Iran's Inflation Tops 27%," Agence France-Presse, September 7, 2008.

"Iran's Khatami Warned About Possible Run for President," Radio Free Europe/Radio Liberty, July 30, 2008.

"Iran's Strategy Is to Confront U.S. Unilateralism: Larijani," Mehr News Agency, June 9, 2008.

"Iran's Unemployment Falls to 10.3 pct—Minister," Reuters India, March 31, 2008.

Islamic Republic News Agency Web site, October 20, 2007, in BBC Monitoring, October 22, 2007.

————, February 26, 2008, in BBC Monitoring, February 27, 2008.

Ja'fari, Mohammad Ali, quoted in *E'temad-e Melli* (Tehran), February 9, 2008, in "OSC Analysis: Iran—IRGC Role in Elections Disputed, Khomeyni Legacy Debated," Dialog/World News Connection 0257851460, February 13, 2008.

Jalili, Sa'id, Islamic Republic of Iran News Network, November 15, 2007, in BBC Monitoring, November 17, 2007.

Jomhouri-e Eslami (Iran), August 20, 2006, in BBC Monitoring, August 30, 2006.

Jomhouri-e Eslami (Iran) Web site, September 26, 2007, in BBC Monitoring, September 28, 2007.

Kamrava, Mehran, "Iranian National-Security Debates: Factionalism and Lost Opportunities," *Middle East Policy*, Vol. 14, No. 2, Summer 2007.

Kamrava, Mehran, and Houchang Hassan-Yari, "Suspended Equilibrium in Iran's Political System," *The Muslim World*, Vol. 94, October 2004.

Kargozaran (Tehran), July 18, 2007, in "OSC Analysis: Revival of Claim to Bahrain Sparks Media Debate," Dialog/World News Connection 0247601137, July 23, 2007.

Kashi, Mohammad Javad, "Iran Paper Says Structure of 'Political Discourse' Undergoing Change," *Mardom-Salari* (Iran) Web site, November 28, 2007, in BBC Monitoring, December 1, 2007.

"*Kayhan* Editor Close to Iran's Supreme Leader Khamenei: 'America and Its European Supporters Must Know . . . That the Price of Supporting [Israel] Will Cost Them the Property and Lives of Their Citizens . . . if the Heads of Some Islamic States Prevent the Muslim Peoples from Attacking the Zionists . . . They Can Be Toppled,'" Middle East Media Research Institute, Special Dispatch No. 1828, January 27, 2008.

Kayhan (Tehran), unattributed report entitled "Ahmadinezhad in a Meeting with 140 Majlis Representatives: Oil Money Must Be Seen on the People's Table," June 21, 2005, in "Selection List—Persian Press Menu via Internet 21 Jun 05," Dialog/World News Connection 0209450646, June 21, 2005.

———, April 3, 2007, in "OSC Analysis: Iran: Hardliners Play Down Opponents' Warnings of U.S. Military Strike," Dialog/World News Connection 0242801514, April 18, 2007.

———, February 3, 2008, in BBC Monitoring, February 4, 2008.

Kayhan (Tehran) Web site, December 3, 2007, in BBC Monitoring, December 5, 2007.

Kemp, Geoffrey, "U.S. and Iran: The Nuclear Dilemma: Next Steps," The Nixon Center, Washington, D.C., April 2004.

Khalaf, Roula, and Najmeh Bozorgmehr, "Iran Ready to Work With U.S. on Iraq," *Financial Times* (London), September 30, 2007.

Khalaji, Mehdi, "Iran's Revolutionary Guard Corps, Inc.," *PolicyWatch*, No. 1273, August 17, 2007.

Khamenei, Ali, "Speech of the Supreme Leader," Vision of the Islamic Republic of Iran Network 1, July 2, 2007, in BBC Monitoring, July 3, 2007.

———, speech in Kordestan, Islamic Republic of Iran News Network TV, in "Iran: Supreme Leader Urges Nation Not to Vote for Those 'Who Submit' to Enemies," Dialog/World News Connection 0280851456, May 19, 2009.

"Khamenei's Leadership Challenged by Mr. Hasan Rowhani," Iran Press Service, February 29, 2008.

Kharazzi, Sadeq, "Comments on the Ahmadinejad Government," *E'temad-e Melli* (Tehran) Web site, March 18, 2008, in BBC Monitoring, March 27, 2008.

"Khorouj-e Akharin Vazir-e Tarafdar-e Eghtesad-e Azad az Kabineh [Exit of the Last Minister Supporting Free Market Economics from the Cabinet]," *Shahrvand-e Emrooz* (Tehran), April 20, 2008.

Kooroshy, Javad, and Farangis Najibullah, "Total Deals Fresh Blow to Iranian Economy," Radio Free Europe/Radio Liberty, July 10, 2008.

Kull, Steven, Ramsay Clay, et al., *Public Opinion in Iran: With Comparisons to American Public Opinion*, World Public Opinion.org, April 7, 2008.

Larijani, Ali, quoted in "We Gave Pearl and Received Bonbon in Exchange," Fars News Agency, November 15, 2004, in "Iranian Daily Says Supreme Leader's Rep Has Reservations About Paris Nuclear Talks," Dialog/World News Connection 0198550647, November 15, 2004.

―――, "Speech at the 43rd Munich Conference on Security Policy," Munich Security Conference, February 11, 2007a. As of August 3, 2009: http://www.securityconference.de/konferenzen/rede.php?sprache=en&id=195&

―――, "Some in Iran Encourage the West to Issue Resolutions," Fars News Agency Web site, June 19, 2007b.

―――, "Interview," *Aftab-e Yazd* (Tehran) Web site, October 21, 2007, in BBC Monitoring, October 24, 2007c.

―――, quoted in *Hamshahri Newspaper* (Tehran) in BBC Monitoring, November 11, 2007d.

―――, "Interview," *Hamshahri Newspaper* (Tehran), November 10, 2007, in BBC Monitoring, December 13, 2007e.

―――, "Comments on Hezbollah," *Tehran-e Emrooz* (Tehran), February 6, 2008, in BBC Monitoring, February 12, 2008.

"Leader Calls for More Efficient Implementation of Article 44 Privatization Plan," Mehr News Agency Web site, Dialog/World News Connection 0249300581, August 26, 2007.

Limbert, John W., "Negotiating with the Islamic Republic of Iran: Raising the Chances for Success—Fifteen Points to Remember," United States Institute of Peace, Special Report No. 199, January 2008.

Litwak, Robert, *Regime Change: U.S. Strategy Through the Prism of 9/11*, Baltimore, Md.: Johns Hopkins University Press, 2007.

Mack, David, Patrick Clawson, Hillary Man Leverett, and Ray Takeyh, comments at "Iran on the Horizon, Panel IV: Iran: What Does the U.S. Do Now?" Middle East Institute Conference Series, Middle East Institute, Washington, D.C., February 1, 2008.

Mahdavi-Kani, Mohammad Reza, quoted in "Head of National Inspectorate Rejects President's Remarks on 'Economic Mafia,'" *Aftab-e Yazd* (Tehran) Web site, Dialog/World News Connection 0261251590, April 22, 2008a.

Mahdavi-Kani, Mohammad Reza, quoted in Shahab News Agency, April 17, 2008, in "OSC Analysis: Iran—Conservative Elders Join in Factional Maneuvering," Dialog/World News Connection 0261401423, April 25, 2008b.

Maleki, Abbas, "Decision-Making in Iran's Foreign Policy: A Heuristic Approach," *Journal of Social Affairs*, Vol. 19, No. 73, Spring 2002.

Mansharof, Y., "Dispute in Iran over Renewing Relations with Egypt," Middle East Media Research Institute, Inquiry and Analysis No. 364, June 15, 2007.

Mardom Salari (Tehran) Web site, November 28, 2007, in BBC Monitoring, December 1, 2007.

Mehr News Agency, November 26, 2007, in BBC Monitoring, November 27, 2007a.

———, December 5, 2007, in BBC Monitoring, December 6, 2007b.

———, December 20, 2007, in BBC Monitoring, December 12, 2007c.

———, February 22, 2008, in BBC Monitoring, February 25, 2008.

Menashri, David, "Iran's Regional Policy: Between Radicalism and Pragmatism," *Journal of International Affairs*, Vol. 60, No. 2, Spring/Summer 2007.

Minou, Delphine, "Ahmadinejad Nomme un Proche sur le Dossier Nucleaire Iranien [Ahmadinejad Names Close Associate on the Iranian Nuclear File]," *Le Figaro* (Paris), October 22, 2007.

"Mohammad Shariati, Advisor to Former Iranian President Khatami, Criticizes Ahmadinejad Government over Foreign, Economic Policy and Support for Hizbullah, Iraqi Militias, and Hamas," Middle East Media Research Institute, Special Dispatch No. 1827, January 25, 2008.

Mohammadi, Mahmud, "Eye on Iran" al-Jazeera, January 18, 2008, in "al-Jazeera TV Hosts Discussion on Iranian Nuclear Power Programme," BBC Monitoring, January 26, 2008.

Moslem, Mehdi, *Factional Politics in Post-Khomeini Iran*, Syracuse, N.Y.: Syracuse University Press, 2002.

Motamed, Arash, "Unsatisfactory Conditions and Imam Mahdi," Roozonline. com, May 19, 2008. As of September 10, 2008: http://www.roozonline.com/english/news/newsitem/article/2008/may/19//unsatisfactory-conditions-and-imam-mahdi.html

Murphy, Kim, "Iran's Guard Builds a Fiscal Empire," *The Los Angeles Times*, August 26, 2007.

Myers, Steve Lee, and Helene Cooper, "Bush Says Iran Still a Danger Despite Report on Weapons," *The New York Times*, December 4, 2007.

Nahavandian, Mohammad, quoted in *E'temad-e Melli* (Tehran) Web site, in "Nahavandian: Moderation in Foreign Policy is the Only Way Towards Development," Dialog/World News Connection 0259100818, March 10, 2008.

Nelson, John Carl, *The Siege of Herat 1837–1838*, thesis, St. Cloud, Minn.: St. Cloud State University, 1976.

"New SCNS Guidelines for Press," Iran Press Service, March 6, 2008. As of September 7, 2008:
http://www.iran-press-service.com/ips/articles-2008/march-2008/new-scns-guidelines-for-the-press.shtml

Nunes, Jesse, "Iran Detains Two on Accusations of Plotting Velvet Revolution," *Christian Science Monitor*, May 23, 2007.

Obama, Barack, "Press Conference by the President," Washington, D.C., February 9, 2009.

Omidi, Hamid, *Kayhan* (Tehran) Web site, September 22, 2007, in BBC Monitoring, September 24, 2007.

O'Rourke, Breffni, "Iran: Ahmadinejad's Threat to 'Traitors' Points to Widening Rift," Radio Free Europe/Radio Liberty, November 14, 2007.

Pollack, Kenneth, comments at "Iran on the Horizon, Panel II: Iran and the Gulf," Middle East Institute Conference Series, Middle East Institute, Washington, D.C., February 1, 2008.

Posch, Walter, "Islamist Neo-Cons Take Power in Iran," Ljubljana Institute for Security Studies, Occasional Paper No. 3, July 2005a.

———, *Iran's Domestic Politics—The "Circles of Influence:" Ahmadinejad's Enigmatic Networks*, IESUE/COPS/INF 0521, Paris: European Union Institute for Security Studies, October 19, 2005b.

———, ed., *Iranian Challenges*, European Union Institute for Security Studies, Chaillot Paper No. 89, May 2006.

———, "Only Personal? The Larijani Crisis Revisited," Centre for Iranian Studies, Durham University, Policy Brief No. 3, November 2007.

"Privatization a Requirement: Rafsanjani," Mehr News Agency Web site, Dialog/World News Connection 0255750745, January 2, 2008.

Quinlivan, James T., "Coup-Proofing: Its Practice and Consequences in the Middle East," *International Security*, Vol. 24, No. 2, Autumn 1999.

Rafsanjani, Akbar Hashemi, quoted by Mehr News Agency, February 12, 2008, in BBC Monitoring, February 13, 2008a.

———, quoted in Voice of the Islamic Republic of Iran, April 11, 2008, in BBC Monitoring, April 14, 2008b.

————, "'Persian Gulf' Is the Historical Name," *Tehran Times*, April 30, 2008c.

Rajanews Web site, April 4, 2007, in "OSC Analysis: Iran—Domestic Media Praise, Criticize Government's Handling of Crisis with Britain," Dialog/World News Connection 0242201037, April 6, 2007.

Rapporteur of the Majles' Council on Security, Iran TV, October 23, 2007, in BBC Monitoring, October 24, 2007.

"Report on Qods Day," Mehr News Agency, October 4, 2007, in BBC Monitoring, October 5, 2007.

"Resistance Led to Great Nuclear Victory," *Tehran Times*, February 27, 2008.

Rezai, Mohsen, "Comments on U.S. Pressure," Esfahan Provincial TV, May 11, 2006, in BBC Monitoring, May 13, 2006.

Rowhani, Hassan, "Farasou-ye Chalesh-haye Iran va Ajans dar Parvandeh-ye Hasteh-ee [Beyond Iran's Difficulties with the Agency Concerning the Nuclear Issue]," *Gofteman*, No. 37, Fall 2005.

————, interview with *Tehran-e Emrooz* (Tehran), BBC Monitoring, December 15, 2006.

————, "Sense of Owning the Country and People, Our Incurable Ailment," *Aftab-e Yazd* (Tehran) Web site, October 11, 2007, in "Iran Cleric Calls for National Unity, Raising 'Tolerance Threshold' to Criticism," BBC Monitoring, October 14, 2007a.

————, interview with *Tehran-e Emrooz* (Tehran), December 13, 2007, in BBC Monitoring, December 15, 2007b.

————, "20 Years Perspectives and a Progressive Foreign Policy," *Persian Journal*, February 28, 2008a.

————, interview with Iranian Student's News Agency, November 22, 2008, in BBC Monitoring, November 27, 2008b.

Roy, Oliver, *The Politics of Chaos in the Middle East*, New York: Columbia University Press, 2008.

Sadjadpour, Karim, "How Relevant Is the Iranian Street?" *Washington Quarterly*, Vol. 30, No. 1, Winter 2007.

————, *Reading Khamenei: The World View of Iran's Most Powerful Leader*, Washington, D.C.: Carnegie Endowment for International Peace, 2008.

Sadr, Sayyed Mohammad, *E'temad-e Melli* (Tehran) Web site, December 13, 2007, in BBC Monitoring, December 17, 2007.

Salama, Sammy, and Gina Cabrera Farraj, "Top Iranian Political Figures Divided Over Nuclear Program," *WMD Insights*, June 2006.

Samii, Abbas William, "It's Who You Know—Informal Networks in Iran," unpublished paper, undated [c. 2004].

———, "Iran's Guardians Council as an Obstacle to Democracy," *Middle East Journal*, Vol. 55, No. 4, Autumn 2001.

———, "Factionalism in Iran's Domestic Security Forces," *Middle East Intelligence Bulletin*, Vol. 4, No. 2, February 2002.

———, "Iran: New Foreign Policy Council Could Curtail Ahmadinejad's Power," Radio Free Europe/Radio Liberty, June 29, 2006a.

———, "The Iranian Nuclear Issue and Informal Networks," *Naval War College Review*, Vol. 59, No. 1, Winter 2006b.

Sanger, David, and Steve Myers, "Notes from Secret Iran Talks Led to Reversal," *International Herald Tribune*, December 7, 2007.

Savyon, A., Y. Mansharof, and L. Azuri, "Iran's Attempts to Renew Relations with Egypt," Middle East Media Research Institute, Inquiry and Analysis No. 426, March 12, 2008.

Sciolino, Elaine, "Iran Pushes Nuclear Talks Back to Zero," *The New York Times*, December 2, 2007.

———, "Iran Paper Offers Clues to Negotiating Style," *International Herald Tribune*, July 22, 2008.

Sepehri, Vahid, "Iran: Political Veteran to Chair Clerical Assembly," Radio Free Europe/Radio Liberty, September 7, 2007.

Shaaki.blogfa.com, "Yek Chah Baray e Takhlih e Ravani [A Well for Mental Offloading]," December 31, 2006.

Shariati, Shaykh Mohammad, "Comments on Foreign Policy," al-Jazeera, January 19, 2008, in BBC Monitoring, January 25, 2008.

Shariatmadari, Hoseyn, "Comments on Influence of the Supreme Leader," *Kayhan* (Tehran) Web site, October 22, 2007, in BBC Monitoring, October 24, 2007.

———, "Iran Paper Analyzes Achievements of Revolution," *Kayhan* (Tehran) Web site, April 2, 2008, in BBC Monitoring, April 4, 2008.

"Shortest Airport Opening in World History," *Iran News* Web site, May 10, 2004, in "Iranian Paper Says Iran's Prestige Damaged by 'Embarrassing' Airport Closure," Dialog/World News Connection 0189100400, May 10, 2004.

Sick, Gary, "Iran: Confronting Terrorism," *Washington Quarterly*, Vol. 26, No. 4, Autumn 2003.

Slackman, Michael, "Iranian Uses Crises to Solidify His Power; Feud with West Fuels Ahmadinejad," *International Herald Tribune*, September 5, 2007a.

————, "U.S. Focus on Ahmadinejad Puzzles Iranians," *The New York Times*, September 24, 2007b.

Sykes, Hugh, "Hezbollah Is Iran's Lebanese 'Aircraft Carrier,'" Ya Libnan, June 9, 2008.

Tabnak Web site, April 21, 2008, in "OSC Report: Ahmadinezhad Speech Sparks Debate on Iran's Economic 'Mafia,'" Dialog/World News Connection 0262750025, May 22, 2008.

Tait, Robert, "Ahmadinejad Challenged for Control of Iran's Economy," *The Guardian* (London), March 7, 2007.

Tajrishi, Payman, "Let Us Not Belittle National Achievements," Iran Web site, December 13, 2007, in "Paper Points Out Iran's International Relations Achievements," BBC Monitoring, December 15, 2007a.

————, Iran Web site, December 15, 2007, in BBC Monitoring, December 16, 2007b.

Tehran-e Emrooz (Tehran), in BBC Monitoring, November 15, 2007a.

————, December 13, 2007, in BBC Monitoring, December 15, 2007b.

Tellis, Ashley, and Michael Wills, eds., *Strategic Asia 2007–2008: Domestic Political Change and Grand Strategy*, Washington, D.C.: National Bureau of Asian Research, 2007.

"The Accuser Is Accused, and Jailed," Iran Press Service, June 11, 2008.

"The Basij Resistance Force," in *How They Fight: Armies of the World*, National Ground Intelligence Center, NGIC-1122-0204-98, 1998.

"The Exposer Is Finally Arrested," Roozonline.com, June 13, 2008. As of August 11, 2008:
http://www.roozonline.com/english/news/newsitem/article/2008/june/13//the-exposer-is-finally-arrested.html

"The Rule of Unmindfuls," Iranian Diplomacy, May 19, 2009.

Tschentscher, Axel, ed., *Iran—Constitution [A Translation of the Constitution of the Islamic Republic of Iran]*, International Constitutional Law, last updated in 1995. As of May 2009:
http://www.servat.unibe.ch/icl/ir00000_.html

U.S. House of Representatives, "Recognizing Iran as a Strategic Threat: An Intelligence Challenge for the United States," Staff Report of the House Permanent Select Committee on Intelligence, Subcommittee on Intelligence Policy, Washington, D.C., August 23, 2003.

Vai'di, Javad, Deputy Secretary for SNSC, Islamic Republic News Agency Web site, February 24, 2008, in BBC Monitoring, February 25, 2008.

Vakil, Sanam, "Tehran Gambles to Survive," *Current History*, Vol. 106, No. 704, December 2007.

Velayati, Ali Akbar, interview with Iranian Student's News Agency, October 22, 2007.

Vision of the Islamic Republic of Iran Network 1, August 27, 2007, in BBC Monitoring, August 30, 2007.

———, January 3, 2008, in BBC Monitoring, January 6, 2008a.

———, March 12, 2008, in BBC Monitoring, March 13, 2008b.

Vision of the Islamic Republic of Iran Network 2, December 4, 2007, in BBC Monitoring, December 5, 2007.

Voice of the Islamic Republic of Iran, February 17, 2008, in BBC Monitoring, February 18, 2008.

Wehrey, Frederic, Jerrold D. Green, Brian Nichiporuk, Alireza Nader, Lydia Hansell, Rasool Nafisi, and S. R. Bohandy, *The Rise of the Pasdaran: Assessing the Domestic Roles of the Islamic Revolutionary Guards Corps*, Santa Monica, Calif.: RAND Corporation, MG-821-OSD, 2009. As of August 4, 2009: http://www.rand.org/pubs/monographs/MG821/

Wehrey, Frederic, David E. Thaler, Nora Bensahel, Kim Cragin, Jerrold D. Green, Dalia Dassa Kaye, Nadia Oweidat, and Jennifer Li, *Dangerous But Not Omnipotent: Exploring the Reach and Limitations of Iranian Power in the Middle East*, Santa Monica, Calif.: RAND Corporation, MG-781-AF, 2009. As of July 31, 2009: http://www.rand.org/pubs/monographs/MG781/

"Where Is This All Going?" Vision of the Islamic Republic of Iran Network 1, December 8, 2007, in BBC Monitoring, December 10, 2007.

"Where Is This Path Going?" *Aftab-e Yazd* (Tehran) Web site, December 8, 2007, in "Iran President's Remarks on Nuclear Programme Useful to Enemies," in BBC Monitoring, December 9, 2007.

The White House, *The National Security Strategy of the United States of America*, Washington, D.C., March 2006.

———, "President Bush Addresses the 89th Annual National Convention of the American Legion," Washington, D.C., August 28, 2007.

Yasin, Kamal Nazer, "Iran: Conservatives Trying to Get President Ahmadinejad to Moderate Behavior," EurasiaNet.org, June 10, 2008.

Yektafar, Babak, "Under the Thinking Cap: A Conversation with Karim Sadjadpour on U.S.-Iran Relations," *Washington Prism*, February 13, 2008.

Zamani, M. P., "Perspective: Airport Controversy Goes Sky-High," *Iran Daily* Web site, May 10, 2004, in "Iranian Paper Says Airport Controversy Takes Iran's Internal Divisions 'Sky-High,'" Dialog/World News Connection 0189100393, May 10, 2004.

Zeidabadi, Ahmad, Roozonline.com, April 23, 2008, in "Ahmadinezhad Speech Sparks Debate on Iran's Economic 'Mafia,'" Dialog/World News Connection 0262750025, May 22, 2008.